Re-thinking Golf
The True-Loft System

By

Richard Berger

Let's have more fun out there....

www.true-loft.com
www.trueloft.org
www.trueloft.club

Published by
Macapa Publishing, Hollywood, California 90068
Copyright: Richard Berger, 2016
Second edition: October 1, 2018

All rights reserved.
No part of this book may be reproduced in any
form without written permission of the publisher.

Printed in the United State of America.
ISBN 978-0-9849364-9-6

Dedication

My original intent was to dedicate this book to Kim Jong Il after I read that he made 18 holes-in-one the first time he ever played a golf course. But then it turned out that it was the North Korean media reporting the event, and they were almost certain to be somewhat too, um, exuberant.

Mr. Kim later went on record saying that his first round of golf only included five aces. I was certainly glad he corrected this as golf, after all, is a gentleman's game.

But then I read about an even more amazing golfing feat and decided to dedicate this book to the holder of that record... one Mr. Gus Andreone of Sarasota, Florida... who, on the 113 yard 14th hole of the Lakes Course at Palm Aire Country Club, watched with unbounded joy as his ball went straight off the tee and into the cup for the eighth ace of his golfing career.

Mr. Andreone was 103 years old at the time. He made the shot and collected $80 in skins from the rest of his foursome. I am in awe of the fact that Mr. Andreone was still out there hustling cash at that age.

The hole-in-one?
Eh.... come on, it was a lucky shot....

Re-Thinking Golf
The True Loft System

By
Richard Berger

Stepping Backwards In Order To Move Forward

What is it about the game of golf that is so compelling? Is it the challenge? Because, make no mistake about it, golf is hard. In spite of the players we watch on TV who make it look easy, it's not easy. Not for us... that vast unwashed horde of weekend warriors who flail away at their local muni, or else some upscale, perfectly manicured torture track with watery graves everywhere... such that after the round you feel compelled to relate to your companions the tale of how many balls you lost.

By the way, they don't care. They're just hoping that your third martini will quiet you down long enough so that they can regale YOU with their own tales of woe.

Possibly it is our expectations that are getting in our way. The golfing public has been sold on the concept that, if you play the same equipment pros play, you can have a similar result. Maybe you can. If you practice as much as they do... Otherwise, don't make me snicker. The golfing public has been sold on many concepts that are not only wrong. but run counter to the original spirit of the game, as:

1) A hard course is a "good' course. The harder it is, the better.

2) Golf is a game for the moneyed classes and it should be expensive and elitist.

In fact, golf is the ultimate democratic sport. It's just you out there with the ball. What YOU do to it determines the result. YOU are responsible, there is no one else to blame. The stories of many of the best players coming from meager circumstances run rampant through golf's history. But the bottom line is this: Golf is a walk in the park... It's you... out in nature, competing against a golf course you can't beat, doing something healthy, taking yourself away from the concrete jungle we live in every day, and putting your body and your mind into a place that cannot but help to lift your spirits.

With all that in mind, I decided not long ago to change my own approach to the game and to try to both simplify it and have more fun while doing it. That is how this book came about. It is part instruction, and partially about the way we use golf equipment. The result has been that I carry less, walk more, don't over-think my game, and play faster.

I have not come up with anything radically new, but instead have used the way golf has been played in the past to re-model the way the game is played now. I'd like to encourage people to get out of that golf cart whenever possible and to be more flexible in their approach to shot-making.

The True-Loft concept promotes the choice of a healthier lifestyle. Walking is good for you, more so as you get older. Swinging a golf club keeps you flexible if you do it correctly. When you're young, your body can absorb the shock of most of the swings we see on the PGA Tour these days. As you get older, that gets harder, and we see the result of that... There are great players that can no longer compete because of injuries.

That "Pro" swing has nothing to do with the average golfer. This book does. It may not be for everyone. It may only find resonance in a niche market... but I think the real niche market is the low handicap, scratch, or professional golfer. There are a lot more of us than there are of them... and we are the engine that propels the game.

The True-Loft system offers the average player the opportunity to reconnect with the roots of the game, use equipment in a way I hope will once again become "fashionable" and to foster the concept that the score is not the reason you're out there...

It's the experience...

Richard Berger
Los Angeles, 2016

Table of Contents

Chapter		Page
Dedication	....	5
Forward	....	7
One	I Pity Tiger Woods.....................................	11
Two	The Mythic Swing......................................	15
Three	Ball Striking...	19
Four	The P.O.N..	27
Five	Aim...	37
Six	The Short Game...	43
Seven	Design Characteristics of Golf Clubs........	51
Eight	Loft Creep...	61
Nine	True Loft..	65
Ten	Playing Shots–The Essence of True Loft..	71
Eleven	Having More Fun......................................	77
Appendix 1	The Etiquette of Rhythmic Play................	85
Appendix 2	Building a Basic Swing	89
Appendix 3	Finding the Impact Zone..........................	92
Epilogue	The True Loft Company............................	95

Chapter One - I Pity Tiger Woods

Golf is a silly game... To become a great golfer has to be one of the most incredibly frustrating things you can do with your life. No matter how good you may get at it, no matter how many low scores you shoot, you're still acutely aware that, if you only made that putt on number 8 or number 10, you know you could have gone just a little lower.

It's a game where the ultimate opponent is the idiot that lives inside your head and, like some long-lost drunken frat brother, he shows up at the most inopportune moments.

I have a stupid question. Why do we bother?

There are many reasons, and we all know what they are. If you've played golf for any length of time, you have your own answers to that question or, *ipso facto*, you would have quit long ago.

For me, getting older, I have come to the sad realization that my best golf is in the rear-view mirror. That is very frustrating at times, but yet another realization is that I still like to get out there and play.

Why? I've been thinking a lot about this over the past few years, and one of my answers can be found in the first sentence on this page. Golf is a game. That means that you're supposed to be having fun.

Unfortunately, one of the things that I've been noticing over the last 20 years or so is that it seems to me that fewer and fewer people actually ARE having fun. Certainly there are far fewer people playing golf than just a few years ago, and fewer young people are taking up the game.

There are many reasons for this, and some of the brighter minds in the golf industry have pointed out that speed of play, pricey greens fees, cost of equipment, and the perceived snobbishness of the game have all been contributing factors. It didn't used to be that way. It certainly isn't that way in many other places where they have played golf for a very long time.

In Great Britain, just for one example, they finish a round of golf in 3 and a half hours. When was the last time you finished a round in under four? One of the reasons for this has to do with where they actually put golf courses. Generally, unlike here, they're built on flat land that is easily walked. Here, many golf courses are built as part of housing developments and almost always, the golf course gets the worst piece of land, meaning that it's fitted into some hilly terrain that requires a cart...and moreover, that course usually winds up being quite difficult because of the forced design and all the uneven lies.

So, over there, they hit, they walk, they hit, they walk...everyone goes to their ball, gives it a whack... and the game goes quickly. And they don't need a cart, something that too many courses here require and is built into the green fee, raising the price. Not to mention that walking is good for you, and if you did it more you could save yourself some trips to the gym.

If you look at old photographs or even paintings of golfers from 100 years ago or more, one thing that usually stands out is that they don't seem to be loaded down with a whole bunch of stuff... you mostly see people carrying small bags with a few clubs, out on the links, hacking away with a piece of hickory... and they seem to be having a good time. Where did that get lost?

The USGA allows you to carry 14 clubs in your bag. And then you probably pile in extra balls, raingear, an umbrella, maybe a ball retriever...maybe a couple extra wedges. I don't know about you, but I used to have so much stuff in my golf bag that I could barely lift it out of my trunk.

Recently I decided to change that. Hence, the "True Loft" system. I'll get to the technical explanations later on in the book, but one obvious immediate benefit is that once I started to make the game simpler, I started to have more fun again... I was able to play quicker, think more clearly about my game, and play many more interesting shots.

And I have come to pity Tiger Woods. Tiger has had the unfortunate experience of being so dialed-in with every shot, so confident of his ability to take on any challenge on a golf course, that, now that his game has him looking like a mere mortal...and what has turned out to be his amazing comeback notwithstanding...I just hope that one day he'll still be able to go out with his buddies, whack a ball around, have a couple of bets, have a couple of beers, and just be glad he's out there. I hope that his expectations don't torture him. I hope that his ability to just have fun doesn't go away. Because golf is a game...

Chapter Two - The Mythic Swing

Golf is a silly game, and it has evolved to a sillier place... Like the dinosaurs who got so big and clumsy that they couldn't compete with smaller, more agile creatures, so golf has evolved to a place where it seems to me to be choking on the overwhelming amount of instruction, equipment, gadgetry, etc. that all promises to "improve your game" if you only go about it using their "methodology of the moment."

Golf is hitting a ball with a stick. Is that simple enough for you? If you want to get any good at it, do it a lot. Empirical knowledge is always the best teacher. Hit the ball with the stick until it goes in the hole.

The golf industry has you convinced that you need special clubs, special balls, special clothes, special range-finders, special ball retrievers, special shoes... special everything, and it's all based around the concept that you're going to hit the ball the same way every time you take a swing at it.

Ha... And double Ha!

Even Ben Hogan, who may have been the best golfer that ever lived, even he said that if he hit two ideal shots in a round, it was a lot. And yet, you've been sold on the idea that you have (lurking somewhere in your inner golfer) this mythic perfect swing that you can call on every time you need a dialed-in 8 iron to go 140 yards to a tight pin, hold the green, and wind up within birdie distance.

You probably only have that swing every once in a very great while, which by the way, is the attraction to this game; that you actually DO have that swing every once and awhile. But the rest of the time you're just trying to survive out there.

And let's even go a little further. Do you want to hit the ball the same way every time? It isn't likely that you do. If you're hitting into the wind, you want to keep it lower. If the wind is behind you, you want to launch it higher than normal. Do you have both of those shots in your bag?

Pro golfers hit balls and play golf every day, and they may even have the EXPECTATION of that mythic swing... but their game is on a whole other level than yours. You do understand that, don't you? So why have you bought into the idea that you should play the way they do? Even pro golfers have the empirical knowledge to know how seldom that mythical perfect swing actually shows up, and so consequently, they're playing the same game you are, except on a higher level. That game consists of three very basic things, in the following order...

1. Ball Striking
2. Aim
3. Short Game

So, if you can hit the ball solidly every time you swing at it, the only other thing is to figure out where it's going to go... hopefully at the target. If it doesn't do that, you need to chip and putt to get your par or bogie (or *other*... insert whatever number you feel is appropriate here).

The real difference between you and a pro is that they turn 6's and 7's into 4's and 5's, and you do the opposite... you turn 4's and 5's into 6's and 7's. When a Pro practices, mostly what they're working on is tempo and alignment... and short game.

Tempo for solid ball striking... the same repetitive tempo will put the fastest place in your swing where you want it... at the ball. Alignment... so you can line up on the target every time and swing the club head at it. (Do I need to explain aim? Possibly. I'll talk more about it later.) And of course, every pro works on their short game until their hands bleed.

So why has this mythic perfect swing become so important? One reason is that it has become the basis for the design of both golf courses and golf clubs, which, in turn, has become the basis for a multi-billion-dollar industry. In reality, while that mythic perfect swing may bear some resemblance to how you might hit a ball off a mat that sits flat on a driving range; it bears very little resemblance to how you hit a golf ball on a golf course. Out there, variations in slope, angle, lie, amount of grass behind, in front of or under the ball... any of a myriad of other conditions come into play on almost every shot, and force you to make all kinds of adjustments in your swing in order to hit that shot.

When you watch the pros on TV, what you see are the guys that are playing well and dialed in on any given week. What you don't see are the guys who are missing greens, scrambling to get up and down, shooting scores that put them somewhere back in the pack but still allow them to make a nice check if they make the cut. And that's most of the rest of the field... just trying to survive.

Your game looks much more like that, if you have a single digit handicap. If not, it doesn't look nearly as good. So why do you buy into the belief that your game might bear any resemblance to the guys that are playing well enough to look like they're dialed in? Clearly, you are delusional... but golf tends to do that to you.

I don't need a caddie to look at a yardage book and tell me, "Ok, Boss... It looks like that pin is cut 9 feet into the front edge. I'd go about a hundred and thirty-eight... take it past the pin and back it up... the front looks like it's a little soft." And I don't need a rangefinder to tell me that the flag is 133 yards instead of 135. I don't need to know that the flag is cut 9 feet on. It just doesn't matter, because far more important than ANY of that information is: "Is the green uphill and how much? How is the wind blowing? Where's my bailout shot?" and whether or not I should go for the flag at all, or just go for a piece of the green.

That's the game I play. How about you? Answer honestly. For the purposes of the discussions in this book, that mythic perfect swing actually hurts not only your enjoyment of the game, but it actually winds up hurting your chances of scoring well because it allows you to believe that your game is better than it really is. And that leads you to trying all kinds of shots that are beyond your ability to pull off. Remember the part about turning 4's and 5's into 6's and 7's? That's one of the primary causes of it.

All of which, by the way, should not discourage you from the PURSUIT of that mythic perfect swing... take lessons, hit balls, work on every aspect of your game. The more you put into your game, the more you'll get out of it, and I applaud you for doing all of it. Just don't start to believe that getting custom-fitted for a three-thousand-dollar set of clubs is a cure for anything. They are custom-fitting you for that mythic perfect swing... and if you're Ben Hogan, you're going to make that swing two times a day. The rest of the time you need clubs that help you get it in the hole and moreover, don't confuse you and tempt you into trying shots you can't hit.

Chapter Three - Ball Striking

Truly we live in a wonderful age...
It's the work of just a few moments to bring up YouTube and look at the swings of almost any great golfer who ever lived. However... You are not likely to be swinging a golf club like any one of them.

An interesting thing for you to do might be to have one of your buddies take out his cell phone and shoot some video of your swing next time you play. If he shoots it from the side (the "caddie" view), you can quickly see your position at impact. This is crucial.

If you look at golfers with great swings, one of the first things you should notice is that almost every single one of them seems to have their eyes focused on the ball at impact. This implies a steady head, and if you want to hit the ball solidly, a steady head is a good thing. Not a frozen head... there are many great ball strikers who exhibit some head movement... but a steady head in terms of connection to your body and the movement of the club.

A couple of other implications of a steady head are:

(a) You will be swinging the club around your spine, letting your hips and shoulders come into play as you turn easily, <u>and</u> it allows for a good finish;

(b) You will be more able to easily transfer your weight from your back to your front foot;

(c) It helps you stay "behind" the ball, and...

(d) It allows you to keep your wrist-cock until later in the downswing, putting your release closer to the ball. *(See figure 1 on the following page.)*

Figure 1 - The Late Release

A few years back I read a physics abstract that talked about the mechanics of the golf swing. The author described the swing as being two pendulums... I had always pictured it as two levers and, not being a physicist, I'm sure his description is more accurate... but the important thing is that you have the rotation of your hips and shoulders supplying the main amount of energy (torque) and your wrists and hands supplying the speed through impact.

If there is any kind of "secret" to golf, it's this...

If the timing of your torque and speed are correct, the fastest place in your swing will be at the ball. There can only be ONE fastest place in your swing, and that's precisely where it needs to be... at impact. This is why tempo is so critical. If you slowly accelerate through the downswing, you stand a chance of reaching optimum speed at impact. If you try to reach optimum speed right from the top, it won't happen. It can't happen. Many other things can happen, but none of those things are any good for ball-striking.

NOTE: *Tempo and timing, while not precisely the same, can be thought of as interchangeable. If you have good tempo, the club will arrive at the ball at the correct time. If you have good timing, likewise.*

There is a very simple way for you to tell if your golf swing is fundamentally sound, and by that I mean whether you're capable of getting the most out of it... It's very simple..

Figure 2 – Throw The Ball

Next time you're at a driving range, pick up a golf ball and throw it. What should instinctively happen is that you should put your weight on your back foot... and, as your throwing arm moves forward, you should push off that back foot and finish the throw with your weight on your front foot. Is that what your golf swing feels like? Now obviously, there are many other things that take place in a golf swing, but if you do not experience the same feeling of weight transfer, you have something basically wrong and you must correct it.

I want to briefly go into the mechanics of the swing for a minute, because obviously, it's critical to playing well. Consider this... You are never going to swing a golf club like Tiger Woods. You're not built like him. If you're old and overweight like me, you might aspire to a swing like Craig Stadler.

The point is, as you probably know, is that everyone's swing is slightly different. All good swings, however, have certain things in common. I'm not going to try to discuss them in detail. Every golf book you ever read talked about the minutiae of swing mechanics... But I would briefly like to mention what I think makes up a good golf swing:

1. A good set-up position that allows you to take the club squarely and smoothly away from the ball AND allows you to swing through to a good finish.
2. A nice shoulder-turn away from the ball that brings the bigger muscles of your body into play so that you don't have to manipulate the club with your hands.
3. A smooth and rhythmic shoulder-turn back to and through the ball.
4. A smooth weight transfer toward the target that creates added momentum and club head speed.
5. Good balance throughout the swing that allows for free movement of the club, but very little movement of your head.
6. A nice release that adds club head speed and squares the face at impact.
7. A full finish that lets your navel end up pointing at or just slightly left of the target because... all other things being equal... where your center of gravity winds up is where you've hit the ball.

Seven things... that's a lot of stuff, and that's what makes golf so hard. It's too much to remember for most of us. So most of us work on one thing, or another, or two of them at a time... We break it down, build it up, rebuild it. And we still don't have it right. Here's why: <u>The golf swing is not a series of positions; every part is connected to every other part</u>.

In order to have a good swing, you have to have a clear idea of what you are trying to accomplish with your swing, and a feel for the continuity of the motion of it. Once you have a clear picture in your mind, it becomes possible to achieve it. And, moreover, that mental picture is necessary because you can't see yourself swing a golf club. You can use video, a swing instructor... but eventually you're on the course alone, and if your swing isn't working, you need to FEEL how to fix it.

Let me give you an example:

If I tell you to throw me a ball, I don't say, "Take your hand back to your shoulder while turning your torso 90 degrees to the right, then cock your wrist at a 45 degree angle that's not quite parallel to the ground, keeping your weight on your right side until you move your arm past your shoulder, then transfer your weight to the left side while releasing your wrist-cock and finish with your palm facing downwards..."

How many times have you heard golf teachers say stuff like this? It only hopelessly confuses you... If I just tell you, "Throw me the ball," your natural athleticism takes over, and you throw me the ball... The fact that I told you to throw it to me lets your natural ability to sense a target take over...and you throw me the ball. Simple.

Remember that mythic perfect swing... it only shows up twice a day... if you're Ben Hogan. My guess is that it shows up because we've cleared a lot of the "turn 45 degrees while shifting the weight, etc." out of our brains and we're allowing ourselves to just swing the club and feel a good tempo. Maybe we swing better when our analytical processes don't get in the way.

Becoming A Better Ball Striker

In order to become a better ball-striker, I think you should do a couple of things:

First of all, find a professional with a similar body-type as your own and find videos of their swing on YouTube. Watch that person swing a club for half an hour. Once you have the picture of their swing implanted in your brain, go out and try to swing a club like that. See what it feels like... have a friend take some video... compare... If it feels comfortable, go hit a few balls. If that feels right, work on developing that swing... Take it to the course.

Secondly, get in the habit of looking at your divot:
a. The direction of your divot tells you the path of your swing.
b. Your divot should start in front of the ball. That means you want to hit the ball before the club hits the ground, thereby compressing the ball and getting the most solid hit.

Thirdly... relax. Eliminate all the tension from your hands, your wrists... In fact, one of the parts of your pre-shot routine should be a tension check. Tension kills speed, and speed, not power is what gives you distance. Check your grip pressure... probably you should lighten it.

The Transition

A critical part of your swing is the transition from backswing to downswing. This change in direction can happen in many different ways, not all of them good. If you watch video of great players, you will notice many variations in the way they do this. One of my favorite golfers for this was Curtis Strange. He seemed to start the club down before he finished getting to the top. It was a silky move I could never imitate.

In any event, the sequence going back is: Hands, Arms, Shoulders, Hips. Coming down, it's the opposite: Hips, Shoulders, Arms, Hands. If you keep to this sequence, the only thing you'll need to worry about is how long you might want to pause at the top before you feel that you are ready to start down. Then, turn your hips at the target in an unhurried way as you slowly accelerate through impact. Don't hurry... wait until you feel ready to start down so your weight shifts forward.

The last thing is to be sure that you're taking the club back into a firm right side (lefties reverse this). That mainly means that you want your weight at the top of the swing to be on the INSIDE of your right foot. The reason is so that you can push off that foot on your downswing and hit into a firm left side. Remember the sensation of throwing the ball? Your instincts took over and you did this without thinking.

If your weight goes to the outside of your back foot, you have to first get the weight to the inside of your foot in order to use it to push

Figure 3. At the top, ready to start down
(Left: Yes, Right: No)

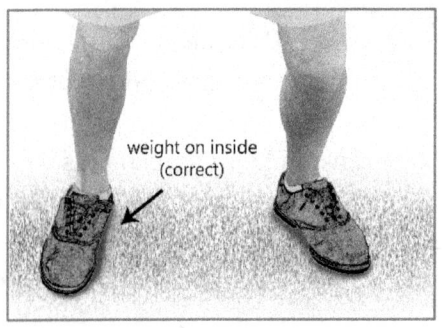
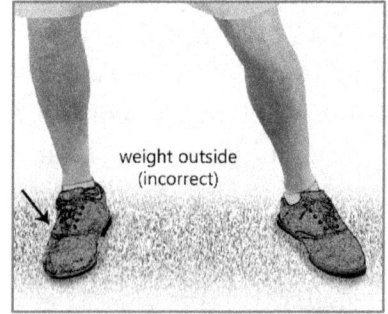

off and transfer your weight to your front foot... and if you don't (or can't) do this... you can't get your weight through the ball, and you can't get to a good finish. So that outside move just makes everything a little bit harder.

<u>AXIOM</u>: *One of the primary causes of mistakes in our swing is putting our body into positions where it has to fight itself during the swing process.*

You can only accomplish one of two things on your backswing: You can either set yourself up for a correct downswing or pull yourself off balance. Guess which is better?

You may find you need a shorter backswing. That's OK. You may find you need a SLOWER backswing. That's OK too... You don't hit the ball with your backswing. You only need it to set-up that correct downswing... and a correct downswing brings you to a good position at impact... producing a solid hit.

Possibly a visual image might be helpful... If you start from a correct position with your chin up slightly, let the rotation of your hips and shoulders bring the club more or less around in a circle whose angle is dictated by the angle of the shaft of that club. In other words, with a driver; the angle will be less steep... with a shorter club, it will tend to be a little more vertical.

Geometry of the Golf Swing

Trying to learn to play golf can be thought of as a mild form of insanity. What drives most of us crazy is the fact that to do it correctly, two very different, unrelated, and more or less opposing motions must be performed at the same time... kind of like patting your head while rubbing your tummy.

The motion can be described simply... You're trying to turn your hips and shoulders around your spine under a steady head... while transferring your weight from your back foot to your front foot during the downswing.

Simple, right? Those of us who have attempted it know better...

The fact that you must restrict your lateral movement (sliding backwards, then forwards) in order to keep one's head steady makes it just a little bit more complicated. Many of us have given up right about at this point.

I can offer this: It IS complicated, but a little patience goes a long way. Once you're clear about what it is you're attempting to do, like practicing scales on a piano... first you go slowly, then you bring it up to speed. Then... suddenly... you feel it and you've got it. And then it becomes second nature and you don't have to worry about it...

Chapter Four - The P.O.N.

Over the years I have watched all sorts of people try to deal with the game of golf with varying degrees of success. I'll admit that I've mostly been amused by the way some people steadfastly twist their bodies into yoga-like positions because they think they want to hit a fade...or a draw...or they're working on the latest swing tip they saw on the Golf Channel.

We make it all so needlessly complicated, and the teachers who talk about it mostly obscure it even further...kind of like politicians who don't REALLY want us to know how they're spending our money, but I digress... Let me try to make it simple.

The Golf Swing is like a pool table. It's all about angles.

Think about it... Correct Angles (all the various angles that your body needs to create in order to produce a square clubface at impact) plus Correct Tempo, WILL square the face at impact with the club on the correct swing-path. It cannot work any other way.

This is not my opinion. This is Sir Isaac Newton's Laws of Physics. You can dispute him. I assure you, smarter people than you have tried and failed.

Once you really start to understand this, your golf swing will no longer be a source of mystery. You will be able to mostly figure it out for yourself. And that's something I believe in very much: Golf cannot be taught... but it can be learned. I believe that's true about a lot of things, by the way: Music, Art, Business, Photography. You can be taught the basics, and people can help you and guide you along the way, but then you need to find your own voice... Same with golf. Ben Hogan said he "dug it out of the ground." That sounds about right to me. But let's talk about angles.

If you take your stance correctly, your hands can hang straight down from your shoulders, encouraging a correct grip and putting you in an ideal position to take the club back into a good position that sets you up for a good downswing.

If the angle of your grip is too strong (or turned too clockwise around the handle), it tends to force your elbows into your side, which will tend to put your club into a closed position at the top and close the face at impact. Too weak, and the club tends to stay open, causing a slice. (*See the Note "About The Grip" at the end of this chapter*.)

If you pull your hands into your body at address, it tends to put the club on a path that is too inside *(figure 4, left)*. If you push your hands away from your body, you'll likely be encouraging your body to take the club too far to the outside *(figure 4, right)*. <u>Every angle you change changes every other angle...</u>

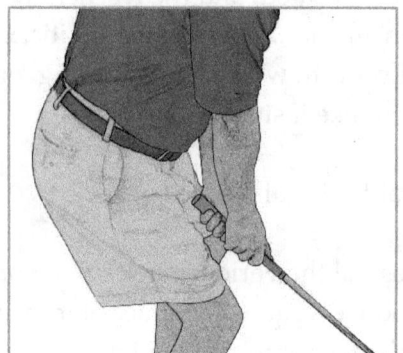 

Figure 4 - Hand Position Angles

Here's the problem... If you've been playing golf for any length of time, you can (and WILL) adapt to almost any swing or set-up defect... It's your natural athleticism taking over and helping you make the club head hit the ball... maybe inconsistently, maybe you'll flub a lot of shots... But once you groove a bad angle into your set-up, most people find that it's easier to adapt to it than go and change it.

One consequence of that, (I've observed over the years) is how hard it is for most people to change a swing once they've played with it for any length of time. Most players, even if they've been working on their swing, or rebuilding it...almost everyone I've ever seen has an instinctive set-up and swing that they revert to under pressure. It takes a lot of work and awareness to change that.

Hogan's line was that "Most people who go to a driving range are reinforcing their bad habits," and I believe that is mostly the case. If you don't go with a plan, and a definite idea of what you hope to accomplish every time you hit balls, what else could you possibly be doing? So... Maybe understanding the PON will be helpful to you.

<u>The Principle of Neutrality</u> (P.O.N.)

Simply put, this means that, all other things being equal, correctly fitted clubs, combined with a square set-up and correct alignment, a correct swing (YOUR correct swing – yes, that's right – your own personal correct swing, and everyone's is different) WILL square the clubface at impact, and the ball will go straight and long and at the target.

It also means: If you monkey around with any of the pieces of what I just described, the ball will wind up somewhere you don't want it. Let me be more specific:

Matt Kuchar and Dustin Johnson both have great golf swings. There are many similarities involved in how they swing the club, but one of the differences is this: Dustin has a much more upright swing, Matt swings flatter, more around his body.

Neither is more correct than the other, both swings are the result of countless hours of practicing what they discovered works best for them. They know how their set-up helps their swing-path... they know the placement of their feet encourages a good shoulder turn... they are aware of many things when they step up to the ball, most of them are not even conscious thoughts because they've been at it so long, but they can feel when it's right or wrong.

The result is a swing that works... for them. For you and I, or any amateur to get to a similar place, we must build our swing from the bottom up and understand how and why it works or doesn't work.

So let's start from the bottom up and talk about what I feel are two of the most important angles in the golf swing... the angles of your feet. In my opinion, there is a critical relationship between the angle of your back foot and the angle of the clubface at address.

Figure 5: Angles of Feet at Address

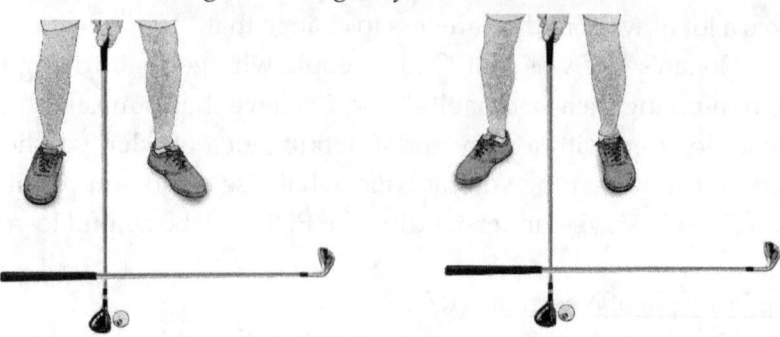

Left: Yes, Right: No

I believe that they must both be perpendicular (or square) to the target line. I have never heard anyone talk about this, but if these angles are not precise, one or more parts of the rest of your swing will have to change to compensate for this.

Figure 6, Back Foot Square

So, back foot square, clubface square on target (and aligned with each other) ...and your front foot should be slightly open (pointed forward). The reason for this can be felt instantly if you stand that way... as if you're addressing a ball (you don't even need to hold a golf club for this) and then, just like you were swinging a club, turn away from the target and back to the target (*figure 6, above*).

If your back foot is square and your front foot is open, you can turn your hips about forty-five degrees to the rear AND... your shoulders can turn so your back is to the target (obviously flexibility plays a role here), or around ninety degrees.

When you turn to your finish, your hips can easily turn to the target and your shoulders can release so that you face forward. If you make the mistake most people make, your back foot will be open (or pointed slightly behind you).

If you do this, and try to turn like a golf swing, you will find that you can turn AWAY from the target very easily, but when you want to turn BACK to the target, your hips will be restricted from squaring up to the target (they'll wind up being pointed right), and your shoulders cannot finish *(figure 7, below)*.

Figure 7

Remember when you threw that golf ball? You instinctively pushed off your back foot and your arm and body moved toward the target. Same thing here... you must be able to move your center of gravity (your hips) TOWARD THE TARGET.

<u>Other Angles</u>

I want to talk briefly about a couple of the other angles that I feel are important. If you have a friend with a video camera or a cell phone, a few seconds of looking at video of your swing can go a long way toward finding good angles and getting you into a good position at impact. And that's all we want, to be in an optimum position when you are swinging through the ball and moving to a good finish.

The Right Elbow

If you look at the swings of most good ball-strikers, you'll see that their right elbow is close to the right side of their body at impact. That's important, but the position of the right elbow at the top of your swing is also important. If you think of a waiter balancing a tray on his right hand *(Figure 8, left)*, that's just about how you should be supporting the club at the top. Coming down, your right elbow can tuck further into your right side *(Figure 8, right)* putting your club on an inside path and avoiding the *coming over the top* move that causes the dreaded slice.

Figure 8

The Left Elbow

I don't believe that you must keep your left arm straight, although many people prefer to teach that and to do that. Many great ball-strikers including John Daly and Bobby Jones, did not play with a straight left arm. HOWEVER... there are two very important things to know... The first is that you must not lose control of the club at the top. This is most evidenced by the left-hand fingers coming off the grip. The second thing is that you must get back into a correct position coming down, so that the left arm straightens out at impact.

Wrist Angle At The Top

If your wrist is "cupped," in other words, bent back like you were pushing someone away from you, it typically opens the clubface at the top. If your wrist is bent down as if you were playing a piano, the clubface will be closed at the top. Neither of these variations are wrong if you are routing the clubface into the correct position at impact. If you are not coming into impact squarely, check either the wrist angle or your timing.

ALIGNMENT ANGLES:

The Neutral Set-up – The Heart of the P.O.N.

At the driving range, put down a ball and an alignment rod or club on the ground pointed at your target. Do everything you usually do to prepare to hit a ball, practice swings, pre-shot routine... all of it.

Now... Step up and place your club behind the ball with the clubface pointed at the target. Adjust the rest of your body so that you are lined up, comfortable and ready to hit the ball... and then freeze... Have a friend take a golf club and lay it on top of your back foot so that it squarely bisects it... In other words, all the angles it makes in relation to the angle of your foot are 90 degree angles.

Figure 9: Bisecting the Back Foot

So, where is that club pointed? It should be pointed at your target, parallel to the alignment club on the ground, but typically it will be pointed to the right *(Figure 9)*.

That's about where your ball is going to go unless you compensate for that angle during your swing. Ok. Let's check the rest of your angles...

Have your friend lay a club on the ground across the line of your toes, touching the toes of your back foot and front foot *(figure 10, left)*. Hopefully, this club is exactly parallel to the club on the target line.

Next, have your friend lay a club across your thighs *(figure 10, right)*. Is that club pointed at the target; is it parallel to the club on the ground? Remember, you haven't moved from your ready position.

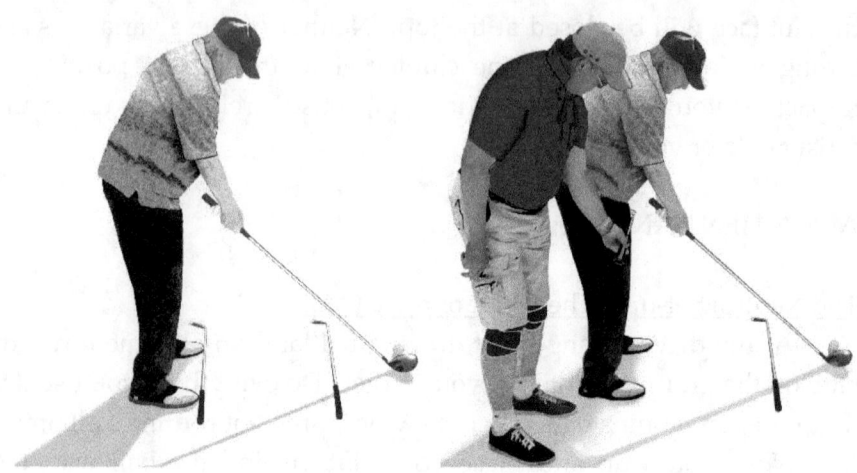

Figure 10: Check feet (above, left; Check hips (above, right); Aligning the shoulders (below)

If the target lines of each check point are not parallel to the club on the ground AND parallel to each other, you need to have a very good reason for it. This is the first piece of the P.O.N. and you want to start with a neutral alignment.

<u>AXIOM</u>: *The most easily fixed and/or controlled part of your golf swing is your set-up. Nothing is moving, and if you know your set-up is correct, you can more easily tell when there is something going wrong during the actual swing.*

If you know that you are set up in a neutral position, and then you go to hit a ball... you can learn a whole lot about your golf swing from watching where the ball goes.

If the ball goes straight... don't fix a thing. If you know you have a neutral set-up and the ball goes right, left, whatever... you can start to dissect the problem by looking first at the angles I've described here... or... if those angles all look correct (and some video goes a long way here), you can start to look for timing errors. Are you starting down too fast? Is the club getting ahead of your body? Is it lagging behind? Are you releasing too early?

<u>NOTE</u>: *...Or... Work out the timing by feel. I actually think feel is easier once you establish what your swing should feel like.*

So, check angles with video, timing by feel... If your set-up is neutral, it will make it a lot easier for you to figure it out. By the way, one last thing about set-up... Your body-type will ultimately determine the adjustments you should make as you arrive at the best swing for YOU. Little tweaks of hand position, angles, even timing... are perfectly OK for you to employ AS LONG AS THEY WORK!

If you start to have swing problems, go back to a perfectly neutral set-up and work from there. *Remember... every angle you change will change every other angle, and...*

1. The only other thing that affects your angles is your tempo.
2. If you set up in a way that is other than neutral, you are creating a demand for much more precise timing coming into impact. In other words, you're making it harder for yourself.
3. Remember the importance of the finish. If you get to a good finish position with your weight on your left foot, you've probably made a good swing because you've kept your balance throughout.

<u>NOTE ABOUT THE GRIP</u>: *The way you hold the club in your hands is crucial to good golf.* I don't want to get too technical here but I will just make the comment that Ben Hogan, in his book *Five Lessons, the Modern Fundamentals of Golf*, devotes the first chapter of about 18 pages just to the grip. The book is only 110 pages total... so you can see that he thought it was important. All golfers should read that book anyway...

I will only say this about the grip:

1. It's important to keep the club in your fingers, not your palms.
2. Holding the club too tightly creates tension in your forearms, which kills speed. You can feel this just by grabbing the club really tightly.
3. No matter which grip you use (Overlap, Interlock, Baseball grip), your palms should face each other.
4. Your hands act as a single unit, neither Right nor Left should overpower.

Chapter Five - Aim
Hitting The Ball Where You Want It To Go

RULE #1: If you are set up correctly, it becomes harder NOT to hit the ball at your target.

In order to understand how to do this, it can be helpful to understand the ball flight laws. They aren't all that complicated. Let's define our terms first:

A *straight* swing path means that the club is moving straight down the target line at impact. It can be straight for a short distance, but the important thing is that the club is moving straight down the line as it moves through the ball.

An *inside* swing path means that (for a right-handed golfer) the club is moving across the target line from left to right as it passes through the impact zone.

An *outside* swing path means that the club is moving across the target line from right to left as it passes through the impact zone.

The Ball Flight Laws work like this:

1. A straight swing path down the target line with a straight clubface at impact will create a straight shot.
2. An inside swing path with a straight clubface at impact will create a draw.
3. An outside swing path with a straight clubface at impact will create a fade.
4. An inside swing path with an open clubface at impact will create a "push" or a ball that goes straight to the right.
5. An inside swing path with a closed clubface at impact will create a hook.

6. An outside swing path with an open clubface at impact will create a slice.
7. An outside swing path with a closed clubface at impact will create a pull-hook.

There just aren't that many combinations, but it sure can get confusing as you try to figure out this game. One problem is timing. We can try for a repeating tempo, but at the club level, most of us have a tempo that doesn't repeat for an entire round. It can vary from hole to hole or shot to shot... and of course, the timing of your swing as it passes through its arc will affect the angles at impact.

One of the reasons that a neutral set-up can be helpful is that it organically gives you a sense of *target*. The importance of everything you do before you swing is critical.

<u>AXIOM</u>: *You cannot overestimate the importance of a correct set-up. Most of your mistakes happen before you ever swing the golf club.*

But bad golfers typically have bad habits... Here's one of the worst: Screwing up your sense of target during your pre-shot routine.

So you choose your club and pick your target. You line it up (or think you're lining it up), then you step up to the ball... it looks like you're ready to pull the trigger... THEN... You take a step or two sideways, away from the ball and start taking practice swings.

You're toast, pal.

Here's why: When you step back in to address the ball, you're no longer aimed at your target and no longer have an idea of where you want your shot to go. You may think that you do, but I'd bet dollars to donuts that way too many thoughts have crept into your head that shouldn't be there.

Practice swings at the side of the ball are a bad habit. If you do it... stop doing it and replace it with a good habit. This is why... first of all, I'm not a big fan of practice swings... What usually happens is this: If you make a good practice swing, you now bring your brain into the process by thinking, "Oh! That was a good swing. I'll just try to repeat it."

Wrong... You won't ever repeat it... Every golf swing is a different experience, it's unique unto itself. No two swings are ever exactly the same. If it's not a good practice swing, the process gets even worse... "That didn't feel right, I'll try to get more turn", or "I'll shift my weight," or whatever... Now you're really lost.

This practice swing from the side of the ball does something else, too. One other really insidious thing. When you step back up to the ball, you are now NO LONGER ALIGNED. Subconsciously, you know it, too. You are no longer sure of where the ball is going to go, and now you have to think about TWO things instead of just one thing: How to hit the ball, and where it's aimed.

If you insist on taking practice swings, do it from behind the ball before you line up. Get loose, feel your tempo, whatever you need to do... THEN, step up to the ball in the way that aligns you to the target, set your club down on the target line, and swing the club. If you do that, you know that your aim is good, and you only have one thing to be aware of: striking the ball well.

Like I said, I'm not a big fan of practice swings... Too often, I see golfers wasting their best swings on air, then they hit the ball badly... I think you should try to just step up and hit it, but it's a *feel* thing, and if you find that a practice swing helps you, OK, but don't do it at the ball.

Just watch the pros... you will hardly EVER see a pro golfer take practice swings from the side of the ball. In fact, I can't even remember the last time I saw one do it. They line it up, step up and hit. One thought in their minds: Hit the ball squarely... And if you do see a pro taking practice swings from the side, they will inevitably step back BEHIND the ball to realign... pick their target... set the club... and hit it. One thought... solid contact.

The only exception might be in heavy rough, where they need to feel the texture of the grass, or a delicate pitch that requires utmost feel, and even then, they will likely get behind the ball to focus on their target before they hit.

I believe in trying to simplify, and aim is a simple thing anyone can learn to do well. There are no moving parts that can go wrong with your aim... unlike your swing. A good pre-shot routine will go a long way toward improving your game. If you have any bad habits in this process, the best way to get rid of them is to substitute good habits.

Don't think that it will be that easy... You'll likely find that you fall back into your old routines all the time as you try to change them. You've spent years teaching yourself to hit a golf ball that way, and it takes work and awareness to do it differently. But if your pre-shot routine isn't actively helping you, it's hurting you.

A pre-shot routine is critical. Hogan used a "waggle". Other players *visualize*... It doesn't matter, as long as it commits you to a target and commits you to the shot and allows you to pull the trigger with total confidence. You need a complete commitment to what you are aiming at.

Harvey Penick had a great line all through his *Little Red Book*... "TAKE DEAD AIM." That's really good advice. Aim small; miss small. The more precisely you can aim at something, the more likely you are to hit it. The more specifically you know what it is, the more clearly you can see it, and the bigger it gets.

Let's take an average tee shot. You stick the tee in the ground, set the ball on it. Then you stand behind the ball, pick your target, step up, and square the clubface. What target did you pick? The fairway? Even the middle of the fairway? Let's be smarter than that. This game can be hard enough. Let's use everything we can to our advantage. Let's start by using the tee box to create the best angle.

Let's say you have a tendency to slice, and there are trees down the right side of the hole. If you tee it up in the middle of the tee box, you haven't helped yourself.

Try this: Tee it up as far on the right side of the tee box as you can, pick a tree or some other marker on the left side of the fairway, well past where you could possibly hit it, and aim for that. Notice the difference in the angle. You have now brought much more fairway into play for yourself, and a much bigger safety zone. If you slice the ball, it still has a good chance of being in play. If by some miracle it goes straight, you're in great position... If you set up in the middle of the tee box and aimed at the middle of the fairway, you'd be in the trees.

<u>Never play a tee shot without thinking about where you want to play your second from</u>, and use the angles you can create at the tee box to help you put the ball in those places.

So, to recap, "Good Aim" is a function of:

1. Picking the best target from where you want to play your NEXT shot.
2. Fixing that target in your mind to the exclusion of ALL ELSE.
3. Taking a SQUARE and CORRECT set-up position that easily allows you to finish your swing with the club head and then your center of gravity pointed at the target.
4. KNOWING that you are truly aimed well. If there is any doubt in your mind about your aim, repeat the process from Step 1.

One more brief thing about why the set-up is important. I started this section by making the statement that: *If you are set-up correctly, it becomes harder NOT to hit the ball at the target.* You say you checked your set-up, it's correct, but you still have trouble hitting the ball where you aim it...

That could be true BUT, by having a neutral set-up position and knowing you are aimed at your target, you've just done one very important thing: *You have eliminated the biggest problem.* Now you know that the ball is not going where you aim it because of an error in your swing path.

I'm a big Ben Hogan fan in terms of his concept of the golf swing. There are people now who say that his concept is a little old-fashioned. It might be true at the professional level. At the club level, I think his concept still stands up. The way he analyzed every part of the golf swing was unrivaled by anyone except Bobby Jones... and he did it in a way that was not overdone.

His concept was simple (there's that word again). There were five parts to the swing: The grip, stance, backswing, downswing, and finish. His process was very logical. Follow this: He felt that if you hold the club correctly, it becomes possible to stand correctly to the ball. If your grip and stance are correct, you can make the right backswing. If those three things are right, it sets you up to make the correct downswing. Get those four things correct, and you can make a good finish. The thing is, if any of those things are incorrect, you will have to make some correction for it during the swing.

Correcting for anything creates a fundamentally incorrect swing and leads to other problems... So I think a good set-up is critical; it gives you two out of the five things, and the finish comes after impact.

So now you only have two <u>other</u> things (the backswing and downswing) to deal with that might be incorrect. Set-up is well worth paying attention to, and because it all happens before you make your swing, you should (in theory anyway) have total control over being able to do it correctly.

One last thing... When you are on a golf course, it's about aim. ONLY about aim. It's not the time to be thinking about technique. Your brain cannot hold two thoughts at once. Work on your technique at the range (where you don't have to think about aim), and come to the golf course ready to focus on your target.

Chapter Six - The Short Game

RULE #1: There is really no way to teach anyone how to chip and putt.

The short game is so much about feel and so little about technique, that I think it's almost counter-productive to talk about it... There is however, one over-riding consideration, and it's this... MAKE EVERY FOUR FOOT PUTT.

This is the magic distance of golf. You encounter four to six foot putts so many times during a round of golf, that you must become comfortable with this distance and good at converting them. If you can do that, you will drop many strokes off your score, and you'll do that very quickly. Anyone can learn to chip the ball into two-putt range - even from fifty yards out - even out of sand; and sometimes you'll chip it close enough for a tap-in. So if you can eliminate any 3-putts, your scores will plummet.

Anyway, since I have to justify my theory about ball-striking, aim, and the short game, I have to tell you something, right? So, here are my short game principles:

1. AIM. Aim really, really, really well.
2. VISUALIZE... Visualize *everything* about the shot. Picture the line, the speed... If it's a chip or pitch, picture where it will land and how it will roll to the hole.
3. Don't let the club head get past your hands until well after impact.
4. BELIEVE you can make EVERY four, five or six-foot putt. Learn how to actually MAKE every four, five and six-foot putt.
5. Develop an accurate feel for distance over uphill and downhill surfaces.
6. Keep the club head moving.

Let's talk about putting first because at least one third of your strokes in every round are putts. You cannot play good golf and putt badly. So, how do you become a better putter?

I've observed basically three different ways that people putt. I don't intend to teach anyone how they should putt (because it is so much about feel and individuality), but I do want to go into these different methods and talk about them in a way that I hope will help enable you to pick the best method for <u>you</u>.

<u>Method One</u> is the most typical, and the one that is taught most often. Stand with your dominant eye over the ball...Place the putter flat on the ground behind the ball. Take the putter back with your shoulders and a pendulum stroke... square back and square through. No breaking your wrists in the stroke (or very little)

<u>Method Two</u> is to stand with your hands very close to your body and use lots of wrist in your stroke in order to *pop* the ball. (This method is usually better on slow greens.)

<u>Method Three</u> is to stand with an open stance with your dominant eye inside the line, using very little or no wrist in the stroke, and to take the putter back square, then stroke the ball down the target line. This method usually allows you a better view of the target line, and if you are having problems finding the correct line, this method may be good for you.

<u>NOTE</u>: *Some very good putters use varying combinations of these three methods depending on the situation.*

Let's talk about *method number one*... Again, just as in the full swing, set-up is critical. Find the line, then commit to the line, then roll the putt on the line you have chosen... A correct set-up makes keeping the putter on line much easier. Do not look at the hole once you've started the putt. Look at the ball... This will stop your head/body from moving and yanking the putter offline.

As you stand looking over the ball, visualize the hole. Fix it in your mind, then, turn your head briefly for one last look at it... then look back at the ball, smooth stroke, listen for the ball to drop. Jack

Nicklaus (who made a few important putts in his day) used to wait until he "saw" the ball go into the hole, then roll back out to his putter before he made his stroke.

Method number two... It happens that I live close to Griffith Park in Los Angeles, home of two pretty good public golf courses... It also happens that Jerry Barber *(PGA Tour Pro and Major Championship winner)* was the head pro there for many years. He used to spend hours on the putting green and pretty much anyone could hang around and putt with him. Many people, including me, took advantage of this.

Jerry was a deadly putter from any distance and he had a very wristy, "pop-py" putting stroke... which was decidedly out of favor by the time I met him. Everyone was trying to be "smooth back, smooth through" at that time.

Jerry tried to get me to change to his way of putting, and it didn't take. Maybe it was peer pressure, or just watching too much golf on TV... but I tried to emulate what I saw all around me, which were players setting up with Method One (above).

When I asked him about why he putted the way he did, he told me that the best putter HE ever saw was Bobby Locke... who had a very strange putting stroke with flying elbows and an unorthodox set-up... but Jerry copied his wristy stroke and it served him well.

So I tried to give that method a fair shot. I experimented with it, but ultimately decided that it wasn't for me. That doesn't mean it isn't for you, especially if you play public courses with slow greens. The greens at Griffith Park were usually cut at Muni speed, or a little on the slow side. I found Jerry's method really useful when I would have trouble getting the ball to the hole.

By the way, one of the better drills I learned from Jerry was the *No Three-Putt* drill, which only had one rule: *Don't three-putt.* If you did, you had to pay everyone playing a quarter (I'm dating myself here)... It didn't matter if you made the putt or not, just don't three-jack it. Someone would pick out a distant hole (it's a big putting green) and everyone aimed for it, and after a while you got pretty good at avoiding the dreaded three putt. It's a drill I still work on.

Method number three... This is the method I use now, with one variation... I sometimes use the "claw" grip. I feel that for me, it allows a smoother stroke. But opening my stance and having my dominant eye inside the line allows me to see the line better when I turn my head to look at the hole... and this creates a better visual image in my brain, which allows me to aim better.

I came to this method after watching footage of Lee Trevino back when he was in his prime and winning majors. He was using an old blade-style putter... maybe a Wilson 8802 (similar to what Phil Mickelson uses now)... and he pulled his left foot way behind the target line, and yet he still managed to create a stroke that was smooth and consistent... and that started behind the ball and went thru it pretty squarely.

I am not in any way suggesting that this is the "correct" way to putt. It is just another variation that you might try if other methods don't seem to be working for you. As you have no doubt seen, there are as many putting methods as there are swing variations out on the PGA Tour... so if one method was truly better, the pros would all be doing that.

But what I would like to see YOU do is to use the method (or come up with your OWN method) that allows you to find the line and roll the ball on the line. Then the only other important thing becomes figuring the speed of the putt.

Discussion of Putting Principles

There are many "Short Game Gurus." I'm a fan of very few of them. If you own any of their books or DVD's, put them away... there may still be hope for you if you haven't yet been totally sold on what they have to say... and they're great salesman because they sound so completely compelling. It's just that I think they're wrong about so many things...

One famous "Guru" has convinced a substantial portion of the golfing world that they should putt so that their ball winds up 17 inches past the hole... not 16 inches, not 18 inches... but 17 inches. His theory is based on the idea of "Never up, never in," and it sounds completely reasonable when you listen to him explain it. But the guy selling you that time-share in Boca Raton also sounded every bit as reasonable and convincing, and how did that turn out again?

He goes on to explain that he bases his ideas about the short game on "scientific" principles... And, in fact, this particular person was a scientist before he took up golf. Therein lies the main problem. Golf involves science, but it is not really a science. It is an art, and the short game is the most artistic part of the game, calling for the most creativity and finesse when it comes to imagining how to get the ball in the hole. When you try to take that and put it in a box of pie-graphs and mathematical tables you are killing any chance you ever have of becoming Mozart, if only for a brief moment.

Okay, Okay; yes, I'm overly dramatic, but I feel strongly about this. Here's the useful part of this conversation...

Bobby Jones, in his book that was written sometime deep in the middle of the last century, had the very same "never-up, never-in" discussion. He had a slightly different point of view:

The Jones point of view was that it was preferable to "die" the ball in the hole. His reasoning was that, when the ball had very little forward speed, you got to use more of the hole... allowing the ball to drop in from the front, both sides, and even the back. And we have all seen this happen whether by accident or design... just as we have all seen putts that were aimed well but moving too fast lip out, skid sideways, etc.

His *further* reasoning was that when you tried to "die" the ball, you became more aware of speed as a critical component of your putt, and that was a good thing, since it demanded more focus.

His *further* reasoning was that when you opted to putt past the hole, you were subconsciously aiming to miss the putt, since a putt past the hole was a hedge against a long second putt... and you were already thinking about your NEXT putt, not totally focused on this one. Bobby Jones won 13 Major Championships using this method. There is really nothing I can add to that.

A shorter backswing can help you with distance control for your putts as well. I have seen many very good putters take a two-inch backswing for a four-foot putt, the logic being that the putter has less of a chance to go offline. It may not be for you. You may need a more "scientific" approach to chipping and putting. The important thing to recognize is that this is the part of the game that calls for the most art and finesse in order to deal with all of the various situations that occur during a round.

The Chipping Conversation

The most important thing for any chip or pitch shot is that you have a definitive plan for the shot. (*NOTE*: *A chip shot has a lower trajectory and typically more "run" than a pitch, which tends to go high and land "soft."*) This includes (but is not limited to) a focused visualization of what you are attempting.

So... after your second shot, your ball is short of an uphill green about 20 yards, with a bunker between you and the putting surface. What are you going to do?

If you have a plan, it may include getting out of your cart with a few clubs: a putter, and some wedges. "Why?" I hear you ask. Because you do not know what you will find when you get to the ball. The very first thing is to look at the lie. Is it fluffy? Tight? Is there a big clump of grass behind the ball? Does the bunker have an elevated lip or is it low enough to play a running shot over it? How much green do you have to work with?

All of these different conditions demand different types of shots with different clubs, and yet, what I mainly see are people getting out of their cart with a putter and whatever club is their favorite for playing around the greens. And that favoritism may be determined by such useless criteria as "I just paid $200 for this wedge and want to try it;" "I like my lob wedge, I hit it well;" "I need to practice my flop shot."

How many times have you ever seen someone go back to the cart and change clubs because they brought the wrong one? Not many, I'll bet... If you're at all smart about this, you'll take a few clubs with you and play the shot determined by the conditions you find when you get to your ball.

Some general chipping principles: Set up with your hands in front of the ball and keep them there until after impact. This is true for 95% of all chipping situations... maybe 99%. Some chipping situations require not only this but also starting with your weight on your left side.

For chipping, the swing happens more slowly, so there is more of a tendency to "peek" before the shot is finished. Keep your eyes focused on the ball until the ball leaves the clubface. If you peek too early, it makes your head move, which will help you top it, hit it fat, skull it, etc.

In general, a good rule of thumb is: *If you are going uphill, take a less lofted club so the ball can run.* A more lofted club will tend to stop once it hits on an upslope. The only exception is when you have very little green to work with. Typically, the grass around the green, being more coarse than the putting surface itself, will stop the ball from rolling onto the green. So always try to land it on the putting surface.

A lofted club requires a much more precise shot. In the short game, distance control is vital. This is usually achieved by the length of your backswing. In a full swing, you're generally trying to hit it as hard as you can, so you make a full turn and take the club back all the way, then accelerate with all speed through impact.

Around the green, a half or three-quarter swing is important to have in your repertoire so you don't decelerate the club at the ball. This is about the worst thing you can do.

So take it back halfway, or a foot, or six inches... whatever the situation demands and accelerate the club through impact... And keep the club moving...

This is particularly important out of the sand. Things change... Different angles, different lies, different distances... And you must be able to deal with them all in a way that aggressively allows you to get the ball in the hole. So...

1. Visualize the shot
2. Pick the spot where you want the ball to land.
3. Create a swing that puts the clubface on the back of the ball.
4. Land the ball on the spot you have chosen.

Big hitters are impressive and intimidating. but chipping and putting accurately and being able to get the ball in the hole is even more intimidating. You don't need me to tell you that you should practice chipping and putting as least as much as you practice hitting full shots.

<u>AXIOM</u>: *The only way you can get good at chipping and putting is to put in the hours of practice you need to develop a feel for many different short-game situations.*

Chapter Seven - Design Characteristics of Golf Clubs

Golf is a game played in three dimensions. At first glance, you may think it's only about distance and direction, but TRAJECTORY is (in my opinion) a very important consideration when you go about choosing clubs to put in your golf bag. So, to my mind, it's important to be able to hit the ball high or low when the situation calls for it. Here are a few common examples:

1. Your tee shot goes off the fairway into the trees.
2. Your second shot needs to go 170 yards to a well-bunkered, elevated green.
3. You have a 165-yard second shot around a slight dogleg to a large, 3-tiered green, open in the front... But the pin is at the back of the green on an elevated third tier, and behind the green is, say, water or OB.

Let's talk about *Number 1* first... You hit your tee shot into the woods. Now what? Well...we've all been there. Let's look at some of the possibilities as we assess the situation...

A. You have a full swing or you don't have a full swing. This is the first thing you have to figure out, as it will determine everything that happens next.
B. Does the lie of the ball allow you to put the clubface on it pretty cleanly, or is the ball covered with vegetation and you didn't bring your weed-eater? The more buried the ball is, the more lofted the club you will have to use.

C. What is your recovery path? Can you knock it on the green? Is there a reasonable possibility that you can advance it down the fairway a good distance? Or, can you barely get it back in play?

D. What is your assessment of the risk vs. reward possibilities? In other words, you have a narrow opening between the trees to the green, versus a much wider opening to merely put the ball back in the fairway. The question then becomes, "How well can you aim?" Or, maybe there is a small tree in your way and you must hit the ball over it. A six-iron gets you to the green, but an eight-iron insures that you can clear the tree... Can you hit that six-iron higher than normal? Keep in mind most golfers delude themselves into thinking they can hit shots that pros can hit... and they can... once out of 10 or 15 tries.

So, clearly, as you try to figure out what to do, having the ability and confidence to control the trajectory of your shot will open up more possibilities. Maybe you need to keep the ball low to scoot it out under low hanging branches. Maybe you need to hit a high hook or a low running fade under and around a tree... And suddenly (if that shot is in your repertoire), you can not only get yourself out of trouble, but aggressively go after your par. For trouble shots, trajectory is vital. OK.

Situation Number 2: In this scenario, you're sitting in the middle of the fairway with 170 yards to an elevated green. The pin is cut close behind a bunker. What do you do? Well, a pro pulls out his seven or eight iron and hits it stiff, but for you it's a three, four, or maybe a five iron. So:

A. If you CAN'T control your trajectory *(in this case, hit it high and land it soft)*, you aim for the open part of the green and either fly the ball there or run it up, but you will avoid the sand and can still 2-putt for your par, even though you're now putting from 50 feet away.

B. If you CAN control your trajectory, you can be far more aggressive and aim at the flag. What's that you say? *You can't hit a four iron high enough?* How about a seven-wood? Maybe you need to start carrying one.

If you watch tournament golf on TV, you probably already understand that this particular situation is one of the things that separates the best players from everyone else. The best players routinely give themselves more opportunities for more makeable birdie putts... And since you don't get on the tour without being an excellent putter to begin with, more opportunities mean more birdies.

The next time you watch a golf tournament, notice how...when a pro player has a long iron shot to a tight pin... they will have exactly the same choice as you: *Do I aim for the fat part of the green and play it safe, or do I try to hit it high over the trouble and land the ball closer?*

Most pros don't carry a seven-wood (some are starting to or else carrying hybrids), and even though everyone is hitting it a lot farther these days, long irons still (relative to the rest of their game) give them problems.

Situation Number 3: In this situation, you may have several choices. Again, a pro wouldn't think twice, he'd just pull out his eight or nine iron and go right at the flag, relying on the loft of the club to go right over the corner of the dogleg and then to stop the ball on the top tier of the green. But, for you, maybe this shot is a five or six iron, and there's more to it. So you need to ask: *Can the club I'm hitting get over the corner of the dogleg?*

A. If it can, and I can get the ball back to the pin, will the ball hold the green and not run off the back into the lake?
B. If I hit it high enough to carry the dogleg, will the ball be likely to have so much spin that it won't release and run up to the top tier, but instead, stay on the lowest level of the green and making a 3-putt a real possibility?

So as you assess this situation... Here's another idea... Hit a low running fade that goes AROUND the corner of the dogleg and still puts enough juice on the ball to carry it up to the top tier... What's that? What's that I hear you whining? *"I can't control that shot. I don't know how to make it stop before it runs off the back."*

That's because you never practice it. That's because when you go to the driving range, you just pound away with your driver and your seven iron. To hit that shot, all you have to do is take a three-quarter swing with a four iron. When was the last time you practiced a three-quarter swing? Did I hear you say never?

One fact that's critical to understand is that *spin creates height*. The thing that gets your ball airborne is backspin. The more backspin you put on the golf ball, the more it will rise... It isn't unlike what keeps airplanes in the air... so... more loft, more backspin.

In a set of golf clubs the thing that is most important in terms of trajectory is the loft of the club. Loft is the angle that aims the clubface from near perpendicular to the ground toward the sky. So in a typical set, those lofts are likely to run from about 10 degrees for your driver to 60 degrees for a lob wedge, with the other clubs being (usually – there is a problem here that I'll talk about later on) made to be proportionally equivalent so you will always have a club that will create the correct trajectory for the shot you want to play. Because...

The more lofted a club is, the more backspin (and the less side-spin) it will put on the golf ball, and the more easily the ball will get up into the air. And, also, the higher you hit the ball, the more it will tend to stay where it lands... and the opposite is true as well. The lower a ball comes in, the hotter it comes in and it will tend to release and run once it lands. This (the backspin/side-spin tradeoff) is also the reason that it is easier for most players to fade or draw a four iron than an eight iron.

One other thing to keep in mind as we talk about this... It's also possible to effectively change the loft of your clubs by changing your set-up. So if you want to keep the ball low, you can play it more toward your back foot and move your hands forward a bit. This will tend to de-loft the face of the club at address, and if you can maintain that position at impact (one of the reasons you need a ¾ swing), you can make your seven iron behave like your four iron. Conversely, if you play the ball more forward in your stance, move your hands back. The ball will tend to fly higher because you've essentially added loft to the clubface.

So, one of the design characteristics we are going to be very concerned with is the loft of the clubface, which, as we discussed, has a great effect on ball flight. Some other things that have an effect on the flight of the golf ball are:<u>Center of Gravity</u>: Where the center of

1. <u>Center of Gravity</u>: Where the center of gravity of the club head is will have a lesser effect on ball flight than loft, but if it is higher on the clubface the ball will tend to fly lower, and vice versa. Also, if the C.O.G. is further back (behind the face) it will tend to produce a higher trajectory.

2. <u>Co-efficient of Rebound</u>: It's really *Restitution*, but rebound is easier... C.O.R. of the material that goes to make up the clubface. The USGA has recently set limits in terms of how "springy" a clubface may be. Most of the manufacturers are pretty close to that limit, but the type of ball you play, your swing speed, how hard you hit, etc., will effect how you should choose what best suits your game.

3. <u>Offset</u>: Offset is the amount of distance that the leading edge of the club is behind the foremost edge of the hosel. If you tend to slice, more offset is usually a good thing. If you tend to hook the ball, you usually want to have less offset.

4. <u>Bounce</u>: Bounce angle is the amount that the trailing edge of the club is higher than the leading edge of the club (irons only), so that when the sole of the club is flat on the ground, the leading edge is somewhat elevated. This is very useful for a sand wedge. *(It tends to keep it moving through the sand.)* And bounce (or lack of it) can also be useful for your other irons, depending on the type of courses you play (tight lies, hard ground vs. fluffy lies, soft turf) and the way that you actually make contact with the ball (hitting down vs. picking it clean).

But the most important part of what affects the overall performance of the golf club, ball flight, and playability, other than loft, is none of these things... It is the shaft. The shaft is to a golf club what the engine is to your car. The body may be pretty, you may have it detailed to a glossy finish, it may reek of money or lifestyle. But if you put the wrong engine in it, it's just going to sit in your driveway.

There are a few things about shafts that you should know. The most important is: *What are the playing characteristics of a shaft, and how can I determine what they are?* And the second question is, of course: *Is this shaft right for ME?*

A golf shaft starts out life as a tapered, cylindrical tube of a pre-determined length. It is up to the club-maker to cut-off parts of it so it will, hopefully, play correctly for you. There is the section at the grip end, known as the *butt*; there is the section in the middle, usually called (surprise) the *middle*; and there is the section at the business end of the club... where the club head is... called the *tip*.

Of the three sections, the *tip* has the most effect on the playability of the shaft...unless you are getting your clubs custom-fitted, in which case, the *butt* end also comes into play because the overall length of the club is very important, and you'll do the final trim at that end.

If you look at a typical steel shaft, what you can see right away is that the shaft has a series of "steps" over most of its length. But down near the club head, there is a section that has no steps, is not tapered *(unless it's tapered on purpose... another discussion for another time)*, and runs smoothly into the club head. This is the tip section of the shaft.

On a graphite shaft, it's the same even though you can't really see it, but that tip section *(which is meant to be trimmed a certain amount, according to the manufacturers spec)* profoundly affects the feel of the club, and if it is correctly trimmed to account for your swing, it will affect your distance and trajectory in good ways. It works like this:

The more of the tip section that you leave at the end, the more flexible that tip section will be, causing the shaft to behave in certain somewhat predictable ways through the swing. What does that mean, exactly?

Well, for one thing, with more *tip*, the club will usually feel *softer*. For another, the ball will tend to fly a little higher. However... It is very important to remember that the people who manufactured the shaft had certain things in mind when they made it, so it usually isn't a good idea to trim a shaft too radically differently from what the manufacturer recommends. That being said...

I must take this opportunity to say that, when it comes to graphite shafts in particular (steel shafts have been around so long that they pretty much have it together), there is no such thing as any kind of industry standard. So one manufacturer's stiff flex shaft may be another manufacturer's regular flex, low-kickpoint may really be mid-kickpoint, etc, etc. It usually comes down to trying it out in the real world.

If you look at the specifications for club heads, you will realize that the longer the iron or the lower the number, the lighter the weight. Usually, each club head weighs around 7 grams heavier than the one before it. So if a 3 iron head weighs 242 grams, by the time you get to the 9 iron, it is going to weigh a little over 280 grams.

And of course, the 9 iron is a much shorter club than the 3 iron so that, supposedly, the club head weight/shaft-length relationship stays consistent (in terms of feel) throughout the set. And if you have a scientific mind, you've already figured out the reason behind this: A shorter club must possess a more weighted head if it is to compress the same kind of shaft in the same way from the longest iron to the shortest…

Compressing the shaft is kind of a catchall phrase that means to *hit it well* (if you didn't know), and that is really what we're after… that sensation of *puring* the golf shot, but consider this for a moment…

You and I go out and buy the same set of Calloway, or Ping, or other OEM clubs off the rack. Let's say that you and I both have the same swing speed, but in terms of how we impact the ball, we are quite different. I have a very smooth tempo, but you have much more upper-body strength and hit the ball very hard. Should our clubs be the same?

According to the general manufacturers specification (which is pretty much based solely on swing speed) for the shaft, we would both be likely to have the same clubs in our bag. Now it's quite possible that one of us picks those clubs up off the rack and they feel like they were made for us. It's unlikely that both of us will have that experience.

For the pros, they will take that same OEM set (that they get paid to play) and make adjustments to every single club in order to fine tune each club in their bag so that they get the most out of it.

When you understand the relationships between the parts of a golf club and your swing characteristics, you will be able to make better equipment choices and get more out of your golf game. Let's look at some of what those swing characteristics are:

1. <u>Swing Speed</u> – by far the most basic and important piece of information for shaft-fitting.

2. <u>Tempo</u> - What is the tempo of your swing? – the second most important piece of information. Are you more like Nick Price or Fred Couples? *Quick?* Or is your swing kind of *Syrupy?*

3. <u>Swing Arc</u> – Do you swing more upright or flatter, more around your body?

4. <u>Dynamic Loading</u> – Where in your swing do you need the shaft to flex, and in what particular ways?

5. <u>Impact</u> - How do you *impact* the ball? Do you hit hard down into it or do you sweep it off the turf? Do you hit the ball or swing the club?

6. <u>Divot Point</u> - Where do you start your divot? Most Pros start their divot in front of the golf ball (meaning they hit the ball before the turf). Most amateurs, this probably means you, start their divot behind the ball (meaning they hit the turf before the ball). *This has a lot to do with how you are releasing the club, a critical component of your swing.*

7. <u>Balance</u> - Are you balanced throughout your swing? This implies a good finish, which usually (not always) means that you have evolved your swing past "hitting from the top."

But the most critical information is the length of the club and the lie-angle. For example, if your wrist-to-floor measurement is 35 inches and your height is 5' 10", your clubs should probably be standard length... or your 7 iron should be 37 inches if it's got a steel shaft and 37.5" if it's graphite.

The lie-angle comes into play if you consistently hit the ball on the toe or the heel of the club. If you hit it out on the toe, probably you want to adjust the club so it's flat at impact and can more easily come into impact with the sole flat on the ground and encourage a more centered hit.

<u>NOTE</u>: *Before you start monkeying around with your clubs, try working on your swing. I believe in a holistic approach, and a correct swing with*

correctly fitted clubs is optimal, but correctly fitted clubs with a bad swing are useless, and vice versa.

Now, keep in mind that the thing we're all looking for in a golf club is that sensation of having the shaft compress at the correct moment in our swing, and we hit the ball like a hot knife slicing butter. This is the precise thing that keeps us torturing ourselves with this stupid game, because once you feel that feeling, you're hooked for life.

So if you were to leave a little more tip at the end of the shaft, the club would play "softer," a little less tip would make it play "firmer." In terms of what is correct for you, I believe that you will arrive at the correct specification through a process of trial and error. A club-fitter can make some educated guesses, but ultimately, there's no substitute for going out and hitting the clubs.

Hit them at the range, play a couple of rounds with them, hit them into the net in your backyard. See how they feel. Personally, I have never used a machine to fit anyone. It's not that I don't think those machines can be somewhat useful, but it just isn't the same as observing how someone uses those clubs in the real world.

Chapter Eight - Loft Creep

If you were to attempt to analyze your golf game in terms of the equipment you're using, how would you go about it? For that matter, how did the clubs you carry in your bag come to be in your bag?

Wait... let me guess... You saw Tiger, or Phil, or Rory... or some other really good player hit those clubs on TV. Or else you liked the fact that their commercials gave you a warm, fuzzy feeling. Or else you went to the golf store and were "fitted" using a computer that did a "comprehensive" measurement of your swing... determining swing speed, launch angle, ball speed, ball spin... all kinds of things. And then you bought the clubs that felt the best when you hit them... off a mat... in a store... after you'd been hitting balls in that stall for half an hour.

Did you (or anyone else) sit down and try to make sense of how you actually use those clubs on a golf course? In the real world? Did you buy those clubs and see an immediate result in terms of you shooting better scores? Did that new driver, the commercials for which promised another 20 yards, actually deliver another 20 yards?

No? OK. Let's try a more rational approach. Here are some random facts and opinions to think about.

1. The clubs you are able to buy bear very little resemblance to the "same" clubs that the pros use on TV. If you go to a PGA professional golf tournament, you will see vans and trucks and mobile workshops from all the major manufacturers. If Rory says that his eight iron doesn't seem to match the rest of his set, there are a small army of people ready to take it apart, tweak it, put it back together. And do it all over again 5 times until he says he likes it. He can likely tell if it's just a little bit off. He hits balls all day long and plays every day.

It's his job. It isn't your job. You play on weekends. For fun. To get out of the house. It's a very different reality.

   2. GAME IMPROVEMENT CLUBS REALLY AREN'T. They're actually "Game-Worsening" clubs. Here's why: They allow you... actually encourage you... to hit the ball with a less-than-correct swing. Back in the old days (B.T. or Before Technology), golfers hit woods made out of ("Gasp!") wood, and the irons (called "Muscle-back irons") had no perimeter weighting to straighten out the ball flight. The only way those clubs worked was to hit them with a correct swing, and so you were constantly subjected to positive feedback when you made a good swing. If you didn't, you could feel that right away too. But it can get even more insidious. If your club compensates for that bad swing, and you keep hitting it, guess what? You're ingraining that swing and making much more work for yourself if you ever want to change to a good swing and shoot lower scores.

   3. If you were to coldly calculate the percentage of good shots vs. bad shots (or let's just say "not-so-good" shots) you hit with each club in your bag, my question would be, "If you only hit a club well once or twice out of five tries, why is that club in your bag?" But yet, most people still may carry a 2, 3, 4, 5 iron around that - by their own calculation - is guaranteed to hit a bad shot most of the time. So why don't you start keeping track of your shots so that you can make an accurate analysis of what clubs in your bag are helping your score, and which ones are hurting it?

   4. Any tour player has an equipment contract, even the guy who's way, way down the money list, and a hat contract, and a shirt deal... and... and... and. And their clubs are tweaked whenever they want. And those warm, fuzzy commercials cost a lot of dough, and the sponsorships, and the "interviews" where guys tell us that they just got a new putter this week that helped them win.

   In other words, there is a whole lot of money riding on who can sell you a golf club with the unstated hope that you'll buy it, and then just drop it in your bag before you run the test of, "Does this club help my score?" Now, it's quite possible, all of that other stuff being said, that you pick up a golf club in a store and hit it, and it feels great, and you hit it really well, and then you take it to the course and keep hitting it well and it DOES help your score. I have no problem with that. The major club companies make some pretty good stuff, and if it works for you, great. Just understand that their focus is not on you. It's on the bottom line. Just imagine what a 30-second commercial during the US Open costs. Someone pays for it.

One thing that is indisputable is something called *Loft Creep*. I think Tom Wishon (an interesting guy who's been in the golf industry many years and has written books and articles about golf equipment) might have coined the phrase, but many people have been aware of this for a very long time.

So how did this come about? It used to be that a Pitching Wedge was 49 or 50 degrees. Today, that's a Gap Wedge. Why do you need a gap wedge? Because, in order to sell you more clubs, the major manufacturers have created a hole in your set where there wasn't one before. There is something called the rule of 24/38. It means that the average golfer has trouble hitting an iron that has less than 24 degrees of loft or is longer than 38 inches. Those numbers used to pretty much coincide with a three iron. Today, a 4 or even a 5 iron is 24 degrees.

So today, when you buy a set of irons that run 3 thru PW, you're getting at least one, probably two clubs you can't hit (the 3 and 4 irons), plus you need a gap wedge because the PW is 44 or 45 degrees and your Sand Wedge is still 55 or 56 degrees. You need hybrids to replace the 3 and 4 irons, a Gap Wedge... You paid for a set, but you almost certainly need to augment the set in order to cover every loft you may need. So... I count two clubs that you paid for, but go in the garage, and three clubs you need to buy to put in your bag. That doesn't exactly seem fair to me.

Why did they go down this road? It's very simple. On Demo Day, when you picked up THEIR six iron and hit it, it went as far as YOUR five iron, and you went, *"Wow! These clubs are great. I'm hitting it a whole lot further with them."* Nope. You're not. They just painted a different number on the bottom.

Chapter Nine - True Loft

I sometimes wonder if, somewhere back in our distant past, when a caveman went out Mastodon hunting and came back empty-handed... I sometimes wonder if some other caveman said to him, "Hey Og. I saw you throw that spear. Is it a glitch in your follow-through or is your spear balanced incorrectly? Maybe that's why you missed."

And then Og replied, "Yeah Bruce. It felt a little off. But what can I do? The spear feels head-heavy, and I can feel that I'm releasing it late."

And then Bruce said: "Well, you could take a lesson from Marty the Mastodon Pro, but it just so happens that I have a brand new Model 29 Hyper-fluxed Hickory Sure-Kill 850 with Advanced Torsion Counterweights right here. It'll give you a better launch angle and at least another 15 yards. I can let you have it at a good discount, too."

I like to think that actually happened. It would explain a lot of things to me.

When I started trying to rethink my golf game, the first thing that occurred to me was that I should try to simply understand my reasons for doing things the way I was doing them. I had spent years experimenting with new equipment, making clubs, tweaking clubs, all aimed toward unlocking the mysteries of what clubs would help me play my best golf...

Even when I was playing my best, only some of all that experimentation did my scores much good. I would still have a good round, a bad round and a bunch of just-ok rounds... Trying to unlock that "equipment mystery" was pretty frustrating.

But I learned something very important... I learned it was important to only have clubs in my bag that I had confidence in. I wanted to know I could hit them well anytime I needed to make a shot. I wanted to have so much confidence in them that I could forget about the club and concentrate on the swing and the shot.

So, one day I went to the range and took all the clubs out of my bag and hit each one ten times. One round of five, then later on, another round of five. So... My results:

Driver: I hit my driver well. I like my driver. Solid contact, good distance. Four out of five shots go where they're aimed.

Three Wood: Hit it well... off a tee. Hitting it off the ground (and by the way – a mat does you very little good here... you need grass to try this), not so great. One or two shots out of five was solid contact and went long and true. The others were varying degrees of a miss.

Five Wood: Solid contact, ball gets up in the air four out of five times. Very comfortable and easy to hit around 200 yards or just a bit more. Mostly goes where I aim it.

Three Hybrid: I stopped carrying a three iron years ago when I discovered the rule of 24/38 and put three and then later four hybrids in my bag. As for this particular club, I can hit it around 190 yards. Hitting it well two or three times out of five. Basically marginal.

Four Hybrid: Solid contact, gets the ball in the air... carries around 170 and rolls out to around 180 or even 185 yards. Hit well three or four times out of five. I can hit it high or low when I need to.

Five Hybrid: Carries 165 and rolls out to 175. Hit solidly three or four times out of five.

Six Hybrid: A "go-to" club. I can hit it high, hit it low, use it out of fairway bunkers. An all-around must club for me to carry. Hit it well around four out of five times. I can carry it 155 to 160 and it will roll out about another five to ten yards.

Seven Iron: I can still hit it 150 yards if I press, but only three times out of five.

Eight Iron: Good out to 140 yards or just a tad more if I press. I hit it well about four out of five times. I sometimes chip with this club as well, or else my...

Nine Iron: Hit it solid 4 out of five times around 130 yards, maybe just a smidge more. I also use it for chipping.

Pitching Wedge: Out to about 125 yards. Hit solid almost always, one of the best clubs in my bag.

Sand Wedge: Can still hit it almost 100 yards. I use it around the green, out of sand.

Lob Wedge: Used to be the most accurate club in my bag, these days I don't have time to put in the practice necessary to be good with it. I can hit it up to 75/80 yards.

So the interesting part of this evaluation is that I could quickly identify at least two or three clubs that were adding strokes to my game. It wasn't an issue of trying to find better clubs to fill those slots... The question became, *"Why did I think I needed them at all?"*

My Three Wood could go, so could my Three Hybrid... likewise, my Lob Wedge. They were costing me strokes, or I was at risk of gaining strokes every time I pulled one of those clubs out. In fact, my Three Wood had cost me two tournaments a few years back when I was in a County league and, on the last par fives, I tried to reach the green in two. I wound up with double bogeys both times, whereas hitting my Five Wood would have meant par or even birdie.

I started breaking things down into yardages. I can hit my Driver 250, I probably average less than that, but sometimes I can put it out there more than that. So what's the next yardage I need? I can hit my Three Wood out to 220... if I catch it clean. But I already know that under pressure, I shouldn't use it. How often do I need that yardage? Well... it turns out that I don't need that yardage all that much. I need 200 yards on most Par fives, but the extra 20 yards isn't much of an advantage, particularly if I can't always count on the club.

Same with my Three Hybrid. I hit my Five Wood 200 yards, do I really need 190? It turns out I don't, not very often. Ditto with my Five Hybrid. My Four Hybrid and my Six Hybrid can cover either a short 180 or a long 160/165. So I took the Five Hybrid out too.

Next to go were my Seven and Nine Irons. It turns out that when I had 150 yards and took out my Seven Iron, more often than not I would come up short. If I took my Six Hybrid and either choked up on it or took a shorter backswing, I was hitting more greens.

My Nine Iron, which I often used to chip, was hard to give up (and I almost didn't) but I can cover with my Eight iron and my Pitching Wedge. It turns out that I don't really miss it after all.

So, more as an experiment than anything else, I started playing with 8 clubs in a small bag: Driver, Five Wood, Four Hybrid, Six Hybrid, Eight Iron, Pitching Wedge, Sand Wedge and Putter. After just a few rounds, I didn't miss any of the other clubs. And something else started to happen. I started thinking differently. Yardage became less important than the kind of shot I was going to play. Club selection was obvious. It became readily apparent when I couldn't reach with a certain club... so I had to bump up two extra clubs and then never had to worry about distance.

Then, I started to think about something else. I started to analyze my new set in terms of the lofts of the clubs, and I realized that I was playing with a throwback set. My lofts (and yardages covered) were:

Club	Loft - Yardage
Driver	10.5 degrees - 235 to 240 (average)
Five Wood	17 degrees - 200
Four Hybrid	22 degrees - 180
Six Hybrid	28 degrees - 160
Eight Iron	38 degrees - 140
Pitching Wedge	46 degrees - 125
Sand Wedge	56 degrees - 100

In the old days, these clubs (by loft) might have had some discrepancies in how they were made, since most clubs were handmade by individuals and most club-makers put their own innovations into their work.

In terms of playability, once hickory was no longer the shaft of choice, that set would likely have been very similar to a set made today, with the caveat that we play on much more manicured courses now. Probably if I was going to design a "Classic" set with today's technology, there would be a couple of tweaks I might make, but, I would do nothing to inhibit the playability of this type of set. And it's eminently playable because it's non-confusing for the amateur player. A pro might have more of a problem, but that's not me.

I noticed something else about the lofts... Back in the old days, most wooden Drivers were 11 or 12 degrees. A Two Wood, which most people couldn't hit, was 13 or 14 degrees. A Three Wood was 15, 16, or 17, Four Wood was 18 to 20 degrees and a Five Wood was 20 to 22 degrees.

Today's technology allows for lighter overall weights and movement of weight around the head, but the lofts were troubling. My Three Wood (which came out of my bag) was actually a Two Wood... No wonder I couldn't hit it well. My Five Wood was closer to a Four Wood, and the rest of my set was also a victim of *Loft Creep*.

Now that I have fewer clubs, I have more choices. Now that I see every shot having more possibilities, I have more confidence. At the distances that have the most effect on scoring, I feel that only having two wedges actually gives me an advantage because I use them all the time.

I chip with my Sand Wedge if I want the ball to go up in the air, if I want the ball to run out along the ground, I use my Pitching Wedge. Using them all the time means I'm practicing with them more, increasing my odds of hitting a good shot.

So I stopped thinking about all of it and now I hit, walk, hit, walk. I think about the type of shot I need to hit instead of the yardage I need to hit it. It's been a minor revelation and has allowed me to get more in sync with the game and have more feel for the golf course. It's been kind of liberating.

Chapter Ten - Playing Shots - The Essence of True Loft

Consider the mind-set of playing golf in a way that makes sure you think in detail about every shot you play... as opposed to the mind-set of seeing a 150 yard shot, grabbing a 7 iron, and blasting away:

With the abbreviated set, since there are far fewer opportunities to *dial it in*, pretty much every shot you have to play becomes much more like a finesse shot... You have to visualize it before you can hit it. This has turned out to be a blessing in disguise.

For the average player, the mental part of the game has always been an issue. How many of us can get on a golf course and truly make the rest of our lives retreat into a distance far enough that we can forget everything and concentrate on the immediate shot? Great athletes have great concentration... this is obvious. And the reality is that this doesn't describe most of us.

But it turns out that the abbreviated set forces us to focus in a helpful way. Because more thought has to go into each aspect of each shot, other thoughts (like: *Where did I leave my sunglasses?* or *Should we try that new Sushi place?*) do tend to fade into the background as we prepare to hit. If we're lucky, by the time we've completed our pre-shot routine and have lined up correctly, we can have total focus on the job at hand... hitting the ball.

I put together my abbreviated set with three basic things in mind. The first was to have clubs in my bag that I have a lot of confidence in, the second was to cover necessary yardages, and the third was to have clubs that had useful trajectories. For me.

I'm not a natural high-ball hitter. Some people are. For those people, they might want to have a slightly different set. They might want a six iron instead of a six hybrid. The lofts of their wedges might be slightly different. I can get a Five Wood up in the air, but it doesn't occur to me to try to hit it over trees. Some people have that shot. I thought about a Seven Wood, but at the end of the day, a Four Hybrid seemed to make more sense because I felt I had more control with it.

I could have put both clubs in my bag. At this point, I certainly have room for them... but that would defeat the purpose in a way. It would seem to dictate that I could "dial in" a certain kind of shot whenever I was faced with it... and I no longer want to do that. I want to consider each shot as a unique, separate entity. I want to find creative solutions if I'm faced with a problem.

I want to go back to the original spirit of the game... playing the ball as it lies and taking what the course gives you. One of the best things about golf is that I feel there is a sense of connection to history. Old photos, paintings, writings, some going back many hundreds of years... all serving to demonstrate that there is something in this frustrating pastime that has a universal appeal.

It might be interesting to take a brief look at the original *Rules of Golf* for a moment... not just to understand how far we've come, but how familiar the game still is. Here then are the Thirteen Original Rules drawn up by "The Gentlemen Golfers of Edinburgh" in the year 1744.

The First Set of Rules For Golf
Articles and Laws in Playing at Golf.

1. *You must Tee your Ball within a Club's length of the Hole.*

2. *Your Tee must be upon the Ground.*

3. *You are not to change the Ball which you Strike off the Tee.*

4. *You are not to remove Stones, Bones or any Break Club, for the sake of playing your Ball, Except upon the Fair Green and that only within a Club's length of your Ball.*

5. *If your Ball comes among watter, or any wattery filth, you are at liberty to take out your Ball and bringing it behind the hazard and Teeing it, you may play it with any Club and allow your Adversary a Stroke for so getting out your Ball.*

6. *If your Balls be found any where touching one another, You are to lift the first Ball, till you play the last.*

7. *At Holling, you are to play your Ball honestly for the Hole, and not to play upon your Adversary's Ball, not lying in your way to the Hole.*

8. *If you should lose your Ball, by it's being taken up, or any other way, you are to go back to the Spot, where you struck last, and drop another Ball, and allow your adversary a Stroke for the misfortune.*

9. *No man at Holling his Ball, is to be allowed to mark his way to the Hole with his Club, or anything else.*

10. *If a Ball be stopp'd by any Person, Horse, Dog or anything else, The Ball so stop'd must be play'd where it lyes.*

11. *If you draw your Club in Order to Strike, and proceed so far in the Stroke as to be e Accounted a Stroke.*

12. *He whose Ball lyes farthest from the Hole is obliged to play first.*

13. *Neither Trench, Ditch or Dyke, made for the preservation of the Links, nor the Scholar's Holes, or the Soldier's Lines, Shall be accounted a Hazard; But the Ball is to be taken out teed, and play'd with any Iron Club.*

John Rattray, Capt

I find a couple of things quite interesting about the original rules. For example:

Rule #1 implies that Golf was originally played not on beautifully manicured, elite courses, but in a meadow, or a field, or some other casual place where people "just got on with it."

Rule #2 kind of implies that right from the very first, there were people who would try to... maybe not exactly cheat, but might try for some sort of advantage.

Rule #3 gets even better. The implication being that someone who hit a bad shot might substitute another ball in a better position. So cheaters were frowned upon right from the get-go. Hence the name: "Gentlemen Golfers" of the society.

Rule #5 gives the first explanation of what we know as a "red stake," or a water or "lateral" hazard, and likewise, Rule # 8 gives us the "stroke and distance" penalty.

In both of these rules, the implication is that you are playing a match with an opponent, which implies that there might have been a few shillings at stake. It also implies the concept of "Match Play," and in fact, we know that golf was mainly played in that way for many years. Tournaments were organized the same way that a basketball tournament is... sixty-four teams playing each other in elimination rounds until you were down to two. It was only with the advent of TV that tournaments started to be "Stroke Play," which tended to ensure that a couple (or even a few) unknowns would not be in the later rounds.

Rule #12 is very interesting, since it speaks to the psychology of the game. If you are further from the hole than your opponent, and you hit a great shot, suddenly the pressure shifts to him. If you happen to be more comfortable with watching your opponent putt first, maybe that can work to your advantage.

It doesn't seem that Golf has changed all that much. Today, there are groups around the world that promote the game played with hickory-shafted clubs. They've gone back to "Gutty" balls... they wear "Plus-fours" and ties when they play. It seems there may be a yearning to rediscover the roots of the game.

In re-thinking the concept of a set of golf clubs, I paid very careful attention to how I might use them on the golf course. Because I had fewer choices, it would be important to have clubs that could cover a wide variety of shots. I would need clubs that gave me distance, trajectory and finesse; and I would need a certain amount of flexibility in the way they could be used. As it turned out, the clubs I wound up with were old-school designs made with modern materials.

Somewhere around about this time, the concept of "True Loft" crept into my head, because that was exactly what I was doing... putting together a set with lofts as they were originally conceived before manufacturers started playing games with them.

I was, by this point, committed to the idea of making pragmatic choices...and I will probably add more tweaks as I continue to play these clubs and my game changes, or I feel the need to adjust either a couple of the distances or the trajectories.

Nothing is written in stone. There are plenty of good club-fitters out there and plenty of good equipment to choose from. What's important is to find and use the equipment that's right for YOU.

Chapter Eleven - Having More Fun

The essence of golf is Man against Nature in the form of Terrain. In other words, it's you against the course, and you can't win. Ever.

Ben Hogan used to say that he dreamed of perfect rounds, where he would make 17 holes-in-one, and then he would dream that the ball lipped-out on 18... and then he would wake up and realize it was always just a dream.

But, all that being said, golf is (in my opinion) the closest thing Western Civilization ever produced that's like Eastern Philosophy:

1. The more you care, the harder it gets.
2. The less hard you try, the easier it is to hit the ball.
3. Like Zen meditation, the more focused you can be, the more clearly you can see the ball and shut all else out of your mind... the ball becomes easier to hit.
4. The less attached you are to the result, the more easily you can embrace the process.
5. The less you think about the score, the more likely you are to shoot a good one.
6. Enlightenment is attained when you find yourself out in the early morning, with some deer grazing at the edge of the fairway, and the only sound you hear are the sounds of birds... and nature... and the sound of the ball hitting the middle of your clubface and then you watch it streak toward the green... and then you look around you and suddenly you realize that you are an integral part of all that; and that you are an integral part of the world. And it just doesn't matter if you sink that birdie putt or not, does it?

Is that fun, or what?

Some of us have very competitive natures, and golf plays right into that in a seductive way. For most of its history, golf was played in a match-play format. In other words, you and I go out on the links, we wager a small (or large) amount of money, and each hole we play is essentially a separate match. I win a hole, I go "1 up." You win the next hole, we are "all-square" again. It didn't matter if I made a Par or a Birdie, or a six, as long as I beat your score. Or, if I couldn't possibly beat your score on a particular hole, I picked my ball up and we were on to the next.

But we would be having a real match, both of us trying our best to beat the other., because we knew that in trying to beat our opponent, we had to dig down and raise our own game.

Any of us who have played competitive sports knows that trying your best to win is just as important as actually winning; and match-play golf gives you a lot of that.

And golf, of course, is the only sport where a real match is possible between players of significantly different skill levels. I have a Handicap Index and Phil Mickelson has a Handicap Index and, consequently, we can play a competitive match based on the number of strokes he would need to give me so we both have a chance to win.

An official Handicap Index is a good thing to maintain if you like competitive golf. The Handicap System offers another spiritual benefit. It quickly shows who the people are who are being less than precisely honest and accurate, and points out those who "play the ball as it lies" and are imbued with the spirit of fair play.

This kind of golf offers, in my opinion, much more excitement than stroke play... where you add up your score at the end and compare it to all the other scores in your group. For players at the pro level, stroke play is a purer form of golf, but unless you're using your score as a measure of spiritual development *(See #6, above)* a small competitive push can keep you focused. If you aren't shooting scores in the 60s, you need to find a different level of golf to satisfy those competitive urges and still give you a little jolt when you feel the flush of victory.

Match play is the answer and, in fact, most weekend warriors have some kind of action that involves a form of match play, be it

Skins, a Nassau, Team bets. It comes down to: "You made your putt for Bogie... If I can sink this 12-footer for par... I win... something..."

And it no longer matters if the real world beat you down that week. You have just redeemed yourself in some small way and your self-confidence got a boost. That's a precious thing in life.

The Mental Game

If you're a sports fan, you appreciate the way that great athletes come through in critical situations. In golf, those situations arise on almost every hole, particularly during match play. How you learn to respond to them is key toward your enjoyment of golf, dealing with the inherent frustration built into the game, and ultimately, the ability to transcend your usual score and shoot a better one.

How can we accomplish that?

In every other sport, making an extra physical effort means carrying the ball those few extra yards for a touchdown, breaking past your man to dunk, or putting a little more juice on that forehand to blow it past your opponent and out of his reach.

In golf, of course, it's the opposite. Making that extra physical effort, hitting harder, swinging faster, putting more power into the shot... any of these almost guarantee a mistimed hit and a mistake. In golf, it's all about self-control and holding back every other athletic instinct that you may have ever possessed... and responding to the challenge at your most relaxed.

So how do you bear down in a pressure situation to make an important shot? Me, I like to visualize Muhammad Ali, "Float like a Butterfly." I like to feel my body get lighter until I'm not really aware of it. I'm only aware of the target if it's a chip or a putt, or for a full shot, I'm only aware of my focus on the back of the ball... and then I can swing the club freely and make good contact.

That's what works for me... You may have a whole other set of feelings, images, or techniques that are useful to you. If you don't, you should develop some.

The thing is, one of the implications of being able to make good shots at the right time is that if you could concentrate at that level for 18 holes, you'd be shooting some low scores pretty much all the time.

At the amateur level, one of the things that separates golfers who score in the 90s or 100s from golfers who can score in the 80s is that, if they hit a bad shot, they can just let it go and re-focus for the next shot.

The pace of the game of golf dictates that you have plenty of time to regroup before the next shot happens. But having that much time between shots also means that our brains can kick in, bringing all our nagging doubts, our hidden fears, our frustrations, our worst anxieties. And, if the course is busy, slowness of play may add yet another layer of torment.

The key to it is being able to forget about it all and rise to another level of awareness. So, as well as settling you in for good ball-striking and target focus, your pre-shot routine should include some way of letting you know that you are mentally prepared to hit the ball.

On the Course

One of the things that drives me a little crazy is watching golfers beat themselves. The game is hard enough. The golf course is usually designed around this principle: Easy bogie, hard par... And yet, day after day, week in, week out, I watch players go to the first hole and immediately walk to the furthest tees. And then their tee shot goes about 200 yards... sometimes straight, more often not.

Whenever I've asked someone why they do that, the answers I've gotten range from delightfully uninformed to just plain silly.

"I want to see the whole course." Yeah, pal. You'll see the whole course all right, including all the gullies, forests, cacti, lakes, and deserts.

"I want to play the same course that the pros play." Are you a pro? No, you aren't. If a hole is 445 yards and you hit your driver 210 off the tee, you're telling me you can hit your Three Wood 235 yards to the green?

"I'm a big hitter." If you're a big hitter and your index is more than 10 or 12, you're just hitting it further into the woods.

"It's the way the designer meant it to be played." Again, no. The designer meant for a hole to be played as a Par 4 (or 5 or whatever.)

If you can't reach the green in two shots, you've just turned that Par 4 into a Par 5. The designer meant the bunkers to be in play. So if your tee shot can't reach the trouble, you AREN'T playing the course the designer wanted you to play. If you aren't close enough to play the approach to the green the designer meant, you're playing a whole other golf course. Play the tees that are correct for your skill level. You'll make more pars. You'll have more fun. You'll play faster and everyone behind you will appreciate it.

We've arrived at a strange place in golf course design lately. Most of the Tour players that have gone into the course design business seem to be building courses designed to impress with their difficulty rather than their playability.

Not being in the business, I don't really know why that is, but I can assume that the idea of a "signature" course must appeal to some people. I guess that this may be in keeping with a marketing strategy given them by a parent company which is likely to be a real estate developer or a resort facility.

Golf course architecture has a long and varied history. From Scottish links courses that may have come about from being routed around the sheep, to Donald Ross, A.W Tillinghast, down to Pete Dye, Billy Bell, Alistair MacKenzie. It's a spectacular list, and it's interesting to note that many courses that were built a century ago have stood the test of time and modern equipment. Most with very little "tweaking".

Somewhere in the last few decades, the definition of a "Hard" course and a "Good" course became muddied. I don't care to name names. But I've played many courses that seemed to me to be designed to frustrate the average player rather than encourage him (or her) to come back and play again.

One course (that shall remain nameless) on the Big Island of Hawaii had some great holes. They were naturally fitted into the landscape, which mostly consisted of red lava rocks that would eat your ball if you hit into them. The problem was that everywhere you needed to hit your ball away from the rocks, that's where some idiot put a bunker. It was a gorgeous looking course, but a silly design. Next day, I played elsewhere.

Course design is easy to understand... A good course is usually laid out from the green back to the tee. In other words, the architect walks the land and figures out where to put 18 greens – where they'll have proper drainage, where they fit into the landscape, where they look attractive... Only then does he figure out the route the golfer should take to get there.

One of the things this process will dictate is the size of the green on a given hole. If you have a small green, do you design the approach so that a golfer needs to use a long iron and carry bunkers to reach it? That's not a good idea because, as you know, a long iron typically comes in lower and "hot" and tends to run after it lands... so a small green dictates an approach with a short iron.

The designer has many tools at his disposal to protect par. Foremost would be distance (length of the hole), then hazards, bunkers, water and the like. If the designer is smart about it, he can configure the hole to allow for *rub of the green* bounces that will always make the hole play differently and always present a challenge. Some designers overdo this, building all kinds of trick mounding around the greens and creating slopes that run off into bunkers.

Golf course design can be thought of in two ways... It is either penal or strategic. The first type of course dictates that if you hit your shot off-line, trouble awaits you... usually of the sort that will cost you at least a stroke or two. The strategic course gives you different options to get to the hole and more chances to hit different types of shots in order to save par. Both types of design are perfectly valid, it all comes down to personal preference. Some golfers like to see the hole laid out in front of them... "I have to hit my tee shot there, then I hit my second there..." Other golfers like to have more options to "think" their way around. The one criteria I believe to be universal is that a golf course should not punish your good shots... It should reward them.

That Which Does Not Kill You Makes You Stronger

When we see golf on TV, what we see is rarely typical of the courses most of us play. We see acres of pure green grass, finely manicured, lush rough...

Your local Muni, with its burned out patches of dirt in the hot summer fairways, can tempt you to yearn for Augusta and that's fine. It can also tempt you to just slide your ball over onto some fluffy grass. I implore you not to do that.

First off, it's the coward's way out. Rule # 4 in the first set of rules pretty much told you that you had to play the ball as it lies. Secondly, if you can learn to hit from a bad lie, when you find your ball with a good lie, it becomes that much easier to hit it well.

Whether it's rough, dirt, whatever, figure out what you need to do, and then just do it. I suppose if you're just learning the game, it might be OK to help your lie a bit, but I think it's a bad habit to get into. If you HAVE to play trouble shots, that's how you'll LEARN to play trouble shots. Just avoiding them is not helpful in the long run.

The Spirit of the Game

In Pasadena, California, in the Norton Simon Museum, there, amidst all the Degas, Picassos, Van Goghs, Cezannes, Rembrandts; there, on an obscure wall, hangs a small painting. It is by a Dutch artist named Aert Van Der Neer. It was painted sometime in the 1600's. That's approximately halfway between Columbus and the Declaration of Independence. The painting depicts a winter landscape and is entitled simply, *A Winter Scene with Figures Playing Kolf.* It depicts a number of people on a frozen river hitting a ball with a stick.

If you search the Internet for similar artwork, you'll find many paintings from the same era that depict "Kolfers" whacking a ball around on ice, on land... one painting even shows a group of 6 people, 4 dressed like gentlemen, with 2 less well-dressed men carrying their clubs, and one of the gentlemen about to hit a tee shot down a fairway.

Who built the first golf courses? No one can be sure, but one thing that came out of that era was the concept that one golf course did not necessarily need to be like another, so golf became the only sport where the playing field changes.

Another by-product of the early age was the idea that, because the playing field was so large, there could not be a referee in the common sense of the word, so the players themselves must be responsible to see that a match adhered to the Rules of Golf.

This idea that golfers must call their own penalties has resulted in some memorable moments in golfing history. On two occasions during US Open play, Bobby Jones saw his ball move slightly as he addressed it. No one else saw it move, but he added a stroke to his score and it cost him one of those championships. Compare that to the next NBA game you watch where the players instantly protest any foul called on them... or professional soccer, where they should give out awards for acting.

All sports reveal character, but golf does it in a unique way. Like other sports, there is the part about meeting a challenge and playing well, but there is also a part where you see your fellow golfers deal with situations that show exactly who they are. And they get to know who you are.

The great paradox is this: If you strictly adhere to the rules, the game gets harder, but you will get better.

APPENDIX I
THE ETIQUETTE OF RHYTHMIC PLAY

BE READY TO HIT WHEN IT BECOMES YOUR TURN

This means that you will be doing your mental preparation while someone else is hitting <u>their </u>shot. You will be thinking about or getting your yardage, looking at the lie of the ball, the line of the putt, figuring out what club to hit, looking at the terrain (uphill or downhill), and <u>most importantly</u>, you will be visualizing the exact shot you need to hit... picturing the ball in the air, picturing what will happen when it lands, how it will roll, etc... so that when it actually becomes your turn to hit, the only thing you will need to think about is striking the ball.

This specifically does NOT mean that you should START your preparation when it becomes your turn. Start during someone else's turn. In Great Britain, if you are on the course for more than 3 ½ hours, they start yelling at you for slow play. They walk, hit the ball, walk, hit the ball... everyone knows what to do, and they do it.

Provisional Balls - If you have ANY reason to believe that you have hit your ball somewhere where it won't be located, into the rough, a hazard, a pile of leaves or any situation where you are not 100% sure you know where it went... HIT A PROVISIONAL BALL!! It takes a second, and when your five minutes are up, you can play on with no BS about it. In fact, you shouldn't even need five minutes to search. Once you get to the area where you hit it, you should be able to tell fairly quickly if you can find it. The only exception is long rough. But you still only have five minutes to search.

CART ETIQUETTE

Park your cart (or leave your bag if you're walking) at the place where you will leave the green. This allows you to clear the green quickly so that the players behind you can hit up. If you have left your cart in order to chip up to the green, you must not leave your cart (or bag) where you will need to walk back toward the players behind you in order to proceed to the next hole. Go get your cart and move it to where you will walk off before you start to putt.

Fill out your scorecard at the next tee. Do not sit at the side of the green while you try to figure out if you took an 8 or a 9. You are making the players behind you wait. Clear the green as quickly as you can. If you've ever been behind someone doing this, you know how annoying it is.

IF TWO PEOPLE ARE IN ONE CART

If you are two in a cart, drop one person at his ball with several clubs, then go to your ball. This makes it easy for you to mentally prepare while he hits. Some people cannot seem to do this. The driver will drive the cart to one ball; the riders will then discuss strategy, which club to hit, etc. They will do it on every shot. That's why they play slow and we get annoyed with them.

DON'T BE AFRAID TO TAKE A FEW CLUBS OUT OF THE CART

If you're mostly keeping your cart on the cart paths, get in the habit of taking at least three clubs with you. The one you think you need, and the ones above it and below it. You won't know which one you'll actually need until you get to your ball. This is particularly true around the greens, where the lie of the ball is so critical. If you get in the habit of having a few clubs with you, you can run it, loft it, bump it, belly it, Texas-wedge it. The point is, you have far fewer options if you only bring one club. You may not always want a wedge. When was the last time you chipped with a seven or eight iron?

AFTER YOU HIT, IT STOPS BEING YOUR TURN

The moment your ball comes to rest, it becomes someone else's turn. That means, once you hit the ball...the next immediate thing you need to do is turn and look at the rest of your foursome to determine: a) Whose turn it is, and b) Where that person is in his routine because *they have been mentally preparing while you hit your shot.*

If that person is about to hit, STOP MOVING... STOP TALKING... BE INVISIBLE. They didn't interrupt you when it was your turn; you owe them the same courtesy. When it is not your turn, you must adapt your play to their rhythm. They should not have to adapt to you. If they want you to mark your ball, tend the flag, move your marker... anything... THEY WILL TELL YOU TO DO IT. Or you can ask if you should. *Don't just do it.* You don't know where they are in their routine, and you might disrupt it.

STAY OUT OF THE OTHER PLAYERS LINE OF VISION

Golf is a game of BALL to TARGET. The more you can focus on the target, the easier it becomes to hit the target. If you distract a player by moving in the vicinity of the target, you can kill that focus. Some people are less bothered by this than others. It is not your place to determine for them what that level is, so walking, talking, moving, twitching, taking practice swings, driving your cart where they can see it, encouraging the cart girl to come over, or anything else that might disturb their concentration on the target, is a no-no.

If you want to pace off yardage, take practice swings, plumb-bob your putt, check the low side, etc. There is usually a way to do it either behind the player's back or in between turns where you won't spoil someone's concentration.

PAY ATTENTION TO THE REST OF YOUR FOURSOME

Get in the habit of frequently looking around to see what the other people in your foursome are doing. Maybe there's something happening that you aren't aware of, maybe someone's hitting out of turn, maybe they need mouth-to-mouth CPR or just drove their cart into a river. If you've ever actually been hit by a golf ball, I don't need to say anything else about this.

IN CONCLUSION

If you get in the habit of doing this stuff, two things will happen. The first is that you will play better golf. Trust me on this. It's such a mental game anyway, and doing all this stuff will go a long way toward improving your focus on the game. The second is that when you're invited to a private club, a member-guest, or a pro-am; or even if you are just paired with good players, you won't embarrass yourself. They will expect you to behave like this. If you don't, you won't be invited again. When all else fails, just think of it like this:

When it's YOUR turn, everyone will wait for you and not disturb you. You should do the same thing in return. Practice the principal of invisibility. You can't go wrong by trying to remain invisible while it is someone else's turn. In return, you have the right to expect that the rest of your foursome will do the same.

APPENDIX II
THE EASY SWING

If the golf swing seems confusing to you, this may be an easy way for you to learn how to do it. The golf swing is very similar to swinging a baseball bat, except a baseball swing is more or less parallel to the ground, and a golf swing is tilted at about a 45 degree angle to the ground. Both swings revolve around the spine with the turning of the hips and shoulders providing the main source of power.

A DRILL FOR APPROXIMATING A GOLF SWING

The simplest way to learn a golf swing (if you are new to the game) is to take a club in your hands with some approximation of a correct grip, and imagine a target.

Stand upright, with your left shoulder (if you are right handed) pointed at your target. Try to line-up your left hip with your left shoulder (also pointed at the target).

Place your back foot squarely perpendicular to the target line, and open your front foot slightly to the target.

Swing the club around your spine on a plane level with the ground, and try to keep your head in one place (like swinging a baseball bat).

When you swing the club back, allow your hands to turn over so that the back of your left hand is pointed at the sky and your wrists are set at a 90 degree angle to your left arm.

When you swing the club to the target, allow your hands to turn over so that the back of your right hand is pointed at the sky.

Try to find a rhythm that allows your hands to lag behind the forward turning of your hips and shoulders, and allows you to hold the angle of your wrists until you can release them at the very end.

Feel the transfer of weight to your back foot when you swing away from the target, and then to your front foot when you swing the club at the target.

Once you feel comfortable with this drill, merely put down a ball, and then tilt your spine at about a 45-degree angle so you can place the clubface behind the ball.

NOTE: *Do not tilt from the waist, but bend forward from the hips so your spine is more or less straight – Not rigid, and you should be relaxed. To further ensure that you're bending from the hips, try this:*

Stand upright with your elbows tucked into your sides, keep your head up, and then bend. You can feel right away if you're bending from the hips or your waist, and if your spine is straight. Your weight is evenly distributed on your feet, not on your toes or your heels. Then the club just rotates around your spine.

Swing the golf club away from the ball, keeping about the same 45-degree angle in relation to the ground.

Turn your shoulders and hips in the same way as you did in the drill, and make sure to transfer your weight to the inside of your back foot, and then... as the club swings forward... let your weight transfer to your front foot.

After you hit the ball, keep the club moving until your hands are over your left shoulder.

That's it... you're golfing...

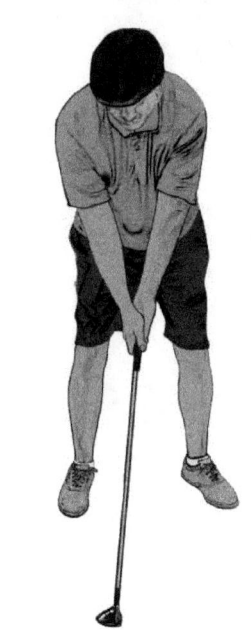

APPENDIX III
FINDING THE IMPACT ZONE

The golf swing is a highly individualized motion, whose purpose is to achieve a desired result, that result being striking a ball in such a way as to propel it toward a target.

As you make the journey from novice to more advanced player, that motion must of necessity, change and evolve. Your physical characteristics (tall, short, thin, heavy, old, young, etc.) will play an important part in the development of the correct swing for you. An older person should not try to swing a golf club like a teenager. You will likely hurt yourself; nor will a heavy person typically have the same kind of flexibility that a thinner person does, so trying to adopt the wrong kind of swing usually has the result of your body being put into positions where it has to fight itself to get to a correct position at impact.

If you understand the P.O.N. you will understand that having all your body angles adjusted correctly will allow the club to swing on the correct path for the shot you're trying to play. The only variable is the position of the ball, and by the way, that can be a huge variable.

Among the many tweaks you can make to your swing, the position of the ball as it relates to your set-up is vital. Because the golf swing is a basically a circle (at least part of one) the part of the arc as it moves through the ball is crucial. You want the club face perpendicular to the target line at impact, and the ball in that spot. Move it toward your back foot a mere inch, your clubface can contact it while still open, causing the ball to go right. Moving it forward the same amount may cause you to come into contact with it after the clubface has started to close.

Ideally, the clubface should come into contact with the ball so that the leading edge of the club (the forward edge along the bottom of the clubface) strikes the ball on its way to coming into contact with the ground. If it's any other club than your driver (more on that later), the angle of the shaft should be leaning somewhat forward, with your hands ahead of the ball at this moment, and the club should be moving along the target line.

"Puring the shot," "Compressing the shaft," "I say, well struck, old chap," or "Whacking the %!#@&! out of the ball," are all meager attempts at describing the sensation of the ball being struck at the correct moment in your swing, in the middle of the clubface, with the club on the correct path... which is what keeps us coming back.

If the club is not moving down the target line, if your release is too early/late, if the angles of your set-up are off... the result will be that your natural athleticism will try to take over to make the club hit the ball... and you will be fighting against yourself to make that correction.

If you take the trouble to work out what your natural swing is, then putting your body in the correct place so that the club has the best chance to impact the ball in the most optimum way is merely a matter of some experimentation. You start by finding the bottom of your swing (or where the club naturally hits the ground) for each club in your bag. That's more or less where the ball should go, and you'll find this may vary a lot.

Bobby Jones had almost a different swing for each club in his bag. Ben Hogan changed the ball position in his stance for almost every club. They were both doing what they figured out would give them the most chances for ideal impact.

They both had radically different looking swings. Hogan's feet were wider than his shoulders. Bobby Jones had quite a narrow stance. No matter; they were doing what was exactly right for them to do in order to get to what they discovered was the ideal impact position; and what happens at impact and the one or two inches on either side of it is the most important part of your swing.

One of the things that taught me a lot was watching the ladies on the LPGA. Since their swings are based more on timing and form rather than strength, they typically will try to maximize every aspect of set-up, timing, correct angles, body rotation, takeaway, and release in order to assure that the most energy is delivered to the ball. You won't be wrong to try to emulate this.

For us amateurs, finding the set-up, swing-path, and ball-placement that gives us the most chances to hit the ball in the middle of the clubface will go a long way toward hitting more consistent shots and enjoying the game more. As for the driver, since we use it so frequently, it's important to be able to hit it straight enough to put it in the fairway. Unlike every other club in our bag, we do not want to hit the ball with a descending blow... we want to take the ball on the upswing, or after the bottom of our swing.

This creates a small dilemma. You will have typically moved the ball far enough forward that the club may be starting to open or close, depending on your swing-path. If you set up with the shaft angle leaning slightly away from the target and your hands slightly behind the ball, you will find that you can more easily swing "up" on it. I like to take the club away "low and slow," and I'll try to come back into impact on the same low path. That works for me. You'll need to find what works for you.

Finding the best impact position is a process. It involves a bit of experimentation, practice, and some patience, and the more aware you are of your set-up and timing, the faster this process will move along. As your swing starts to evolve, those impact positions may change. After a while, it will all become second nature. You'll step up to the ball, set your club down behind it, adjust your body to the target line, and swing away freely... knowing the ball is headed right where you want it to go.

EPILOGUE
THE TRUE LOFT COMPANY

It has occurred to me that there may be enough people that appreciate what this book is about to start some kind of company to make equipment that fits our concept. If this ever happens, the True Loft Company will be dedicated to connecting golfers to both the history and simplicity of the game of golf. Our philosophy of golf equipment is simple... If any one particular company made a club that was truly more accurate or gave you more distance, it's obvious to us that all the golfers on the pro tours would be using that particular club, or that particular brand of club.

Their living depends on hitting a golf ball as long and as straight as possible.

Think about that the next time you see a TV commercial or a full page ad in a national golf magazine for a particular brand of club. Think about how much that ad costs, how much the company is paying professionals to play their particular brand, how much the marketing of their products costs...

And then think about this...

Every year, those same companies promise that their NEW products will hit the ball further, straighter; with MORE spin; with LESS spin; hit it HIGHER, LOWER. They promise you that if you buy their clubs, you will be buying a better game and lower scores.

You cannot buy a better game.

You can only improve your game by improving your golfing skills. Those skills include your swing, course management, your short game and your own self-confidence in your ability to execute the shots that you visualize.

One thing that will help you visualize the shots you need to play well is to get out of that cart and walk the golf course. In walking, you absorb your surroundings subconsciously in ways that taking a cart does not allow, and, it changes the pace of your concentration on the game.

Suddenly you find that you have more time to think about the shot you need to hit, and more time to prepare to hit it in exactly the way it needs to be hit.

It is our opinion that a bag filled with 14 clubs (some people carry even more) gets heavy after only a few holes, and furthermore, that bag likely contains clubs that you don't have complete confidence in.

We say, "You don't need them all."

We're aware of how crazy that sounds. But yet, only carrying clubs you have total confidence in will improve your chances of hitting a good shot. "But wait," I hear you say: "What happens when I only have an 8 Iron and a Pitching Wedge and I need to hit a shot that goes the distance of my 9 Iron?"

The answer is simple. After a very short adjustment period, you will become comfortable hitting the ball a little longer or shorter (depending on the situation) and will find you are still able to make your par if you hit the ball at the target. And you will be more likely to do that because you will be using the clubs in which you have the most confidence.

There is of course, a very simple way to find out if you are comfortable playing with only 7 or 8 or 9 clubs.

Try it.

My own experience has shown me that the clubs I'm using now are a good mix for me, even though I would not consider them "ideal". There are a few "tweaks" I might make in order for me to feel that the distances, the club lengths, the lofts and lie angles are precisely what I need.

I have even toyed with the idea of designing the precise set I want. You can check the website occasionally to see if I really do this. But that's all beside the point. The point is to keep your best clubs in your bag, take out your marginal ones, and walk the golf course. Golf is a game for a lifetime. Once your knees give out for tennis, soccer, racquetball... almost every other sport... long after that you'll still be able to walk a golf course, breathe fresh air, and either hack a ball around with your buddies or be making new friends.

That's what I love about golf.

Richard Berger

Los Angeles, 2016

www.true-loft.com
www.trueloft.org
www.trueloft.club

ABOUT THE AUTHOR

When I started playing golf, there were a bunch of local teachers, plus all kinds of books you could buy, video tapes (Yep...we still used tape back then, even Beta tapes... ask Grandpa about that one, whippersnapper), as well as the usual assortment of "golf aids" that were basically on the market because golfers, like fly fishermen and home beer brewers, will buy almost anything.

So I took some lessons with a few different teachers with the result that I was more confused than when I started out. Maybe I didn't find the right person, maybe I didn't hit enough balls at the range (I hit a lot of balls); whatever the reason, I wasn't making progress.

One day I happened by a yard sale and saw this old book by someone called Ernest Jones. It was called "Swing the Clubhead." I remember thinking, "How much more obvious could you be? Of course you're swinging the clubhead.." On the inside, there were a few pictures of a golfer swinging a handkerchief with a jackknife (remember those?) on the end of it. My initial reaction was, "What the heck does this have to do with golf?"

It seemed like a really silly thing to do until I tried it.

And... in a sudden flash of an almost divine epiphany, the importance of tempo in the golf swing was revealed to me. And then I started to make real progress.

That book made me very curious about how the game was taught in the past, and it lead me to reading books by other past luminaries until I finally discovered Bobby Jones and Ben Hogan, and I studied what they had to say until I almost wore the print off the page.

I feel that I had the two best golf teachers that ever lived, and indeed, digesting what they had to say started me on the way to being able to shoot some pretty good scores and understanding the golf swing in a much deeper way. Between them, they won 22 Major championships, and their knowledge of every aspect of the game is, in my opinion, unrivaled... even more so because of how articulately they were able to express themselves and pass that knowledge along to us.

Today, we live in an age of golf technology. We have spin monitors, putting coaches, video cameras, computer simulations, range finders. I'm sure that it's all useful at some point, but I question the value of a lot of it when it comes to recreational golfers. I have yet to see a golf book that tried to make the game simpler. Not everyone wants to take golf so seriously. We want to go out with our friends and have a good time. If we play well enough to be able to hit more good shots than bad shots, have a chance to win a couple of bets, bond with our friends and not embarrass ourselves... that's fun.

And that's the point.

Richard Berger
Los Angeles 2016

Richard Berger is a semi-retired writer, musician, and videographer who has lived in Los Angeles for many years. "I didn't start playing golf until I was almost 40," he says, "and I've tortured myself with it ever since." He keeps looking for some healthful outdoor activity to take up as a substitute, but isn't ready for lawn bowling quite yet. "And the dress code seems to be even stricter," he laments. His other interests include virtual mountaineering, music, and vinyl repair. He has played in the same Thursday golf group for many years. "We bet small amounts of money and argue about who should collect. Now that we're all getting older and more forgetful, the arguments are getting even more entertaining."

SOME SHOUTOUTS

People I would like to thank who made this book possible...

Al Krever, who in a very real way has turned a bunch of pages into something that people might actually want to read.

Fraser Heston, who casually said to me one day, "Why don't you write a book about your theory?" He probably didn't think I would rise to the bait, and he probably regrets speaking now.

Roger Towne, for his notes and who kept me from over-writing this.

Jerry Miller, my golfing buddy of many years, who I know feels very sad about the fact that my game has deteriorated more than his over the decades.

The models who kindly posed for the photos inside: Jerry Miller, Roger Towne, Jack Heston, Vladimir Velasco, and Fraser Heston. Thank you for being my friends.

Laurie Post, who did the artwork and final layout. You really outdid yourself.

And, most importantly, Tova Laiter, my best friend and companion for 30-odd years who still doesn't really understand that I can watch golf on TV and still write. So there.

www.ingramcontent.com/pod-product-compliance
Lightning Source LLC
LaVergne TN
LVHW051508070426
835507LV00022B/2994